Bissell • **Newhott**

University of California at Irvine

Education and Training for Tomorrow, Inc.

Guide to the Internet in Educational Psychology

Madison, WI Dubuque Guilford, CT Chicago Toronto London
Mexico City Caracas Buenos Aires Madrid Bogotá Sydney

ISBN 0-697-37158-1

Printed in the United States of America.

10 9 8 7 6 5 4 3 2 1

contents

preface

"Instead of doing the lesson plan, I decided to do the Internet project. I worked with another classmate . . . it's amazing how much information was available to us through the Internet and the World Wide Web. The topics that we chose to research were motivation, cooperative learning, teacher expectations, prior knowledge and elementary education.

We found plenty of information on the topics we chose. . . . [At first] the searches were difficult because we were both somewhat Internet illiterate. We didn't know how to get into Netscape, and we didn't know where to begin . . . I learned a lot. For example, I became pretty much Internet literate. I can now go into a computer lab and access most any sites on the World Wide Web myself . . . the information that's available through the Internet is so phenomenal. And all of it is so helpful!"

Senior, University of California, Irvine
Fall Quarter, 1995

This *Guide to the Internet in Educational Psychology* is designed to prepare future educators to be literate users of the Nation's rapidly expanding Information Superhighway, the Internet. This extraordinary system of computer networks allows users to communicate with and access information from people, organizations, and databases around the world.

The *Guide* reflects an expectation for higher education: that it will increasingly involve students in exploring sources of knowledge from the Information Superhighway in conjunction with their use of textbooks in the academic disciplines. This is necessary in order for students to share in both the fundamentals of a field and the most current developments within the knowledge base. It emphasizes that, in the Information Age, inducting students into a field means helping them master two types of knowledge: fundamental paradigms and concepts, which are relatively stable components of the knowledge base, and current knowledge, which is constantly changing and is now accessible to all.

It is essential to create instructional materials that will be valuable resources for students for years to come and that will enable them to acquire new knowledge on a continuing basis. This is what we have attempted to do in creating this *Guide* to accompany the rich coverage of concepts in educational psychology found in *Educational Psychology: Windows on Teaching* by T. Crowl, S. Kaminsky and D. Podell and *Educational Psychology: Effective Teaching, Effective Learning* by S. Elliott, T. Kratochwill, J. Littlefield, and J. Travers.

The motivation to create the *Guide* was in part influenced by the strong interest in using the Internet as part of their course work expressed by students in educational psychology classes. It was the students' belief that university classes should be taught using the technologies of the 21st century.

The vast majority of students enrolled in educational psychology courses will pursue careers in the field of education. Increasingly, they recognize that the majority of *their* students will be more experienced in advanced technologies than they themselves, and this troubles them. Exploring the Internet as part of their educational psychology courses can help them substantially to become proficient users of it and of the World Wide Web, a graphics-oriented part of the Internet that provides links to text, images, sounds and video. Learning about these resources early and using them throughout their professional preparation opens endless, challenging learning and teaching opportunities for future educators and for the K-12 students whose knowledge and whose views of knowledge they will shape.

This *Guide* is designed to be used in conjunction with the user-friendly **Educational Psychology Home Page** that Brown and Benchmark has created on the World Wide Web. The **Home Page**, consistent with the nature of the "Web," is designed to be continuously updated and expanded to reflect new resources and developments in the field of education.

The **Educational Psychology Home Page** provides "point and click" access to most of the resources described in the *Guide* and to many other valuable resources for future K-12 educators. It also contains the fundamental tools needed for searching and exploring the Internet. In addition, it includes frequent updates about (a) the field of education and (b) high quality resources accessible through the Internet or electronic mail (e-mail). It identifies Internet resources that relate to central topics in the Brown and Benchmark educational psychology texts. In addition, both the *Guide* and the **Educational Psychology Home Page** have been designed to be well-suited for use with most other basic and advanced texts in educational psychology and related fields.

I want to express my deep appreciation to colleagues in the University of California, Irvine Department of Education who have created a culture emphasizing the critical role of technology in the preparation of future educators. The shared commitment and support for focusing on state-of-the-art educational technologies in our teaching and research facilitated significantly the preparation of this *Guide*. I am very appreciative of the time devoted by both Henry J. Becker and Karen Ivers to reviewing the *Guide*. I also want to thank Andy Burchett and Ali Mela, who identified resources included in the *Guide* and Anna Manring, who contributed significantly to the *Guide's* preparation and editing. I want to express my considerable gratitude to Sue Pulvermacher-Alt, Managing Editor, and Suzanne Guinn, Developmental Editor, at Brown and Benchmark, who supported the project throughout. Finally, it was my husband, Stanley Newhoff, whose knowledge of the Internet contributed significantly to conceiving the project and the *Guide*, and whose guidance and support were critical to their development.

Quick Steps for Using the Guide and the Educational Psychology Home Page

Symbols Used in the *Guide*

Shaded boxes contain useful information.

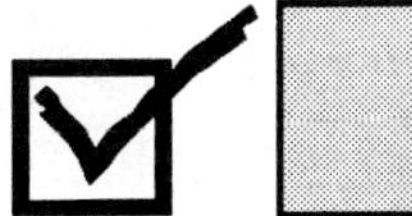

A shaded box next to a check mark contains sequential steps for accomplishing a specific task.

A home page pointer icon opposite an Internet address in the text indicates that the site is accessible directly from the Brown & Benchmark **Educational Psychology Home Page**.

E-Mail Only: Quick Steps

This is for individuals who have access to e-mail but not to the World Wide Web or other Internet resources. There are still many ways you can use the *Guide* as a supplement to *Educational Psychology*. Find out how to use e-mail on your campus computer or with your commercial service provider (e.g., America Online). Read *How Electronic Mail is Used for Communicating and Accessing Resources on the Internet,* Part 2 of the *Guide*. Then:

1. Start your computer.
2. Establish a connection with your communications network (i.e., your campus network, local Bulletin Board, etc.).
3. Open your e-mail software (e.g., Eudora).
4. Send a message to one of the resources accessible via e-mail suggested in the *Guide* and listed in the Site Index at the back of the *Guide*. Follow the instructions provided via return e-mail.
5 If you have any questions about how to use the *Guide*, send a message to:

edpsych@tmhe.com

The Internet: Quick Steps

If you have access to the World Wide Web, use it to connect with the **Educational Psychology Home Page**. The **Home Page** provides easy access to Internet resources in education. Find out how to activate the Web browser available through your Internet service provider (i.e, your campus computer center or commercial service provider) or another source. Then:

1. Start your computer.
2. Establish a connection with your Internet service provider.
3. Open the Web browser software (Netscape, Mosaic, etc.).
4. In the "Location" or "Netsite" dialogue box at the top of the screen, type the address of the **Educational Psychology Home Page**:

   http://www.bbp.com/edpsych.html

5. Press Return or Enter.
6. Begin exploring the **Home Page**.
7. Use the search engines (EINet Galaxy, InfoSeek, Lycos, WebCrawler, or Yahoo) to search the Web.
8. If you have questions about how to use the *Guide* or the **Home Page,** send an e-mail message to

   edpsych@tmhe.com

Note: Many of the Internet addresses provided in this *Guide* occur at the end of sentences. Do not mistake the period ending the sentence for a dot at the end of the address.

part

1

What Is the Internet?

The Internet is a vast, world-wide system of interconnected information and communication networks. Because of the quantity and quality of the information available online, and the ease of communication regardless of distance, the Internet is widely regarded as the most promising resource for strengthening the nation's K-12 education system.

The Internet contains hundreds of thousands of documents, resources, databases and projects relevant to K-12 education. The vast majority of resources on the Internet are free. Many of the education resources can help future teachers develop a keen understanding of the foundations of learning and prepare for future roles as facilitators of challenging and meaningful learning experiences. Active scholars will find the Internet an invaluable adjunct to traditional data sources.

There are currently more than 30 million people connected worldwide through the Internet. It is projected that there will be 100 million people online by 1998. Thousands of K-12 teachers worldwide have already discovered the extraordinary value of this growing Information Superhighway. No matter what education field you currently teach or plan to teach, you need to become a proficient user of the Internet.

History and Overview of the Internet

The Internet began as a computer network developed by the U.S. Department of Defense in the 1960's and 1970's for transporting research data. By 1986, the National Science Foundation had built upon this foundation to establish a high-capacity data transfer network that permitted researchers associated with the nation's supercomputer centers to communicate data and messages. This became the foundation for the Internet.

As the Internet evolved, other networks were allowed to connect to it, resulting in today's configuration — the world largest network of computer networks, connecting computers in over 175 countries. All of the connecting computers use common communication protocols. This has enabled communication and information exchanges to grow exponentially among universities, government agencies, research organizations, businesses, and individuals.

Until the end of 1993, the Internet's often cryptic commands and primarily text-based capabilities limited its utility as a large-scale educational resource. The nature of the Internet has changed dramatically during the past few years and its utility for K-12 education has expanded enormously. There are now dozens of user-friendly navigation tools and close to a million readily-accessible resources for current and future K-12 teachers, including extensive materials for students in educational psychology and virtually every other subject area.

The Internet Today

Advances in software for navigating the Internet have made its vast potential accessible to large numbers of college and university faculty and students and to increasing numbers of K-12 teachers. Most importantly, the World Wide Web, known as the "Web," with an innovative authoring system, has facilitated the creation of millions of documents that contain not only text, but also graphics, video clips, and sound. "Web browsers," which are very simple to use, enable users to explore the entire Web, clicking on and accessing items of interest located on computers throughout the world.

For K-12 educators, the Internet provides digests of educational research, "state-of-the-art" newsletters, research articles, curriculum ideas, lesson plans, a wide variety of learning and teaching resources, active learning projects, and online access to user groups having interests similar to their own. It offers infinite new possibilities for future K-12 teachers and their students. It enables them to expand their knowledge and to participate in new modes of learning that involve exploration of the most current information sources and communication and collaboration with other learners throughout the world.

Most computer and communications experts anticipate that the Internet will quickly become the primary communication medium of our civilization — for families, businesses and industries, and educational institutions. It is possible that the Internet and the services provided through it will ultimately redefine television and many print publications, including the daily newspaper. The Internet is the fastest growing form of mass media in history. Notably, for the very first time, U.S. sales of computers for household use have now exceeded sales of televisions for household use.

Visualizing the Internet

What metaphors and images might be used to enhance understanding of the Internet and its vast set of resources? A good place to begin is with telephone networks. Consider the revolutionary advances that resulted from Alexander Graham Bell's invention of the telephone. Consider what it meant for individuals suddenly to be able to talk and exchange information with others located at any site to which their phone line could be connected.

The Internet represents a revolution at least as significant. It has built upon and expanded the capacity of the extensive network of telephone lines and intercontinental satellites used to transmit phone messages so that text files, data, graphics, pictures, video, and audio can now be communicated to locations throughout the world. Using the same transmission systems, every form of information can now be shared — from one person to another, between individuals and groups, among groups of individuals — and the exchange occurs immediately on the Internet.

In visualizing Internet sites, it is useful to use the metaphor of a worldwide electronic community. Internet sites can be compared to large cities, small cities, rural areas, town halls, stores, shopping centers, schools, universities, libraries, individual homes and farms, and the like. Each of these is inter-connected with every other via a telephone network, and communications are transmitted along high-speed digital lines and regular telephone lines.

Many of these Internet sites have their own "electronic libraries" of resources which they share freely with others. Most are continually expanding the contents of their electronic libraries. Some sites allow users to browse the contents of their electronic libraries; others enable users to take away copies of materials in their libraries. Some have created connections between resources in their libraries and related resources. "Point and click" connections enable individuals to go directly to these additional resources. Others invite users to contribute materials to their electronic libraries. This extensive web of interconnected resources is an extraordinary tool for enhancing understanding of such subjects as educational psychology, teaching, and learning.

Using the Internet

One of the most important attributes of the Internet is the relatively low cost of using it and accessing the multitude of resources on it. To use the Internet, an individual needs a computer, a modem, communications software, a phone line, and an Internet service provider. None of these things is difficult or expensive to acquire. The vast majority of computers are suitable for using the Internet; computers with greater internal memory are necessary for using the World Wide Web. Modems differ in their speed — the bits per second (bps) at which information is sent. One with 9600 bps or more is needed to capture pictures or sounds as well as text and to use the Web.

After ensuring that you have the necessary equipment, the next step you take in becoming an Internet user is determining what direct Internet connection or Internet service provider will be used. Online connection to the Internet can be established through direct Internet providers such as most colleges and universities, through independent Internet service providers such as CERFnet and NETCOM, through some bulletin board systems, or through commercial online services such as America Online, CompuServe and PRODIGY.

Colleges and universities frequently serve as direct Internet providers. They provide their faculty and students with user-friendly tools for electronic mail and for navigating the Internet. Commercial online services also provide easy-to-use operating software (generally for both Macintosh and PC systems) for both purposes. Through any these "Internet Gateways," users can communicate on and access the resources of the Internet.

Once you have established your Internet service provider, the steps to becoming a confident user are relatively simple. The easiest way to begin exploring the educational resources on the Internet is to start with a *Web browser* such as Netscape or Mosaic and begin visiting valuable sites on the World Wide Web and elsewhere on the Internet. The remaining parts of the

Guide will take you through this process. The sites included have been selected because of their relevance and quality.

The **Educational Psychology Home Page** has been developed in conjunction with this *Guide* and can serve as your primary Internet interface. The **Home Page** can be accessed easily by any computer that has Netscape or any other software program for browsing the World Wide Web. To connect with the **Home Page**:

1. Establish a connection with your Internet service provider.
2. Open a Web Navigation Tool (Netscape, Mosaic, etc.).
3. In the Netsite location box, enter the Web address for the **Home Page**:

   http://www.bbp.com/edpsych.html

4. Press Enter or Return.

From the **Home Page**, thousands of resources pertinent to education and educational psychology are accessible by selecting items from its menus.

If you will be using the *Guide* with e-mail as your primary tool, you will still be able to obtain significant amounts of information regarding education and educational psychology. Throughout the *Guide*, instructions and e-mail addresses are given for this purpose. In general, they require that you:

1. Establish a connection with your communications network or Internet service provider.
2. Open your e-mail software (Eudora, PopMail, etc.).
3. In the "send to" location, enter the e-mail address for the resource cited in the *Guide*.
4. Send a message indicating what you would like.

One note of caution: Much of the Internet is still under construction and many of its sites are experimental. You will inevitably encounter delays, "Could Not Connect" messages, frozen screens, and names and addresses that changed just before you logged on. Just take it all in stride and persevere. It's worth it. Welcome to cyberspace — the new frontier.

part

2

Using Electronic Mail for Communicating and Accessing Resources on the Internet

Communication occurs on the Internet and resources are located on it through various different types of Internet networks. These are accessed through different Internet tools. To use our earlier metaphor, we can envision the different parts of the Internet as places (countries, cities, neighborhoods) we want to visit and the tools for getting there as different modes of transportation. The tools serve basic communication and navigation functions and generally are available in a number of software options. Service providers (colleges and universities, America Online, etc.) typically make available to the individuals using their Internet connections one or more software options.

Electronic Mail

Electronic Mail Addresses

Individuals communicate on the Internet through electronic mail (e-mail), sending and receiving mail via their Internet addresses. When you set up an account with an Internet access provider, you select or may be given an e-mail address. It usually consists of some variation of your name, followed by the "@" sign, then the designation for the computer or service you are connected to and its type (for example, "edu" for education or "com" for commercial). The information after the "@" sign is known as the Internet *domain* where you receive e-mail. Your e-mail address, plus whatever password you select, is your passport to the Internet.

Increasingly, colleges and universities provide their faculty and students no-cost or low-cost e-mail accounts on the Internet. An example of a student e-mail address would be *istudent@myuniv.edu.*

E-mail addresses for students and faculty typically contain: their first initial and the first several letters of their last name; the first several letters of their last name only; or an identifying code of numbers and/or letters. This is the individual's user identity ("user id") on the Internet. The domain (after the "@" symbol) specifies the location of the computer and is typically the Internet designation for the particular college or university. The user's address may specify one or more "within institution" designations, such as departments or projects, each followed by a period (referred to as "dot") before the college/university designation. Then, the e-mail address ends with "edu," the domain designation for educational sites on the Internet. An example would be *iprof@gse.myuniv.edu.*

In order to understand recipients' addresses when sending or receiving e-mail communications, it is important to understand the concept of "domains" on the Internet. Domains refer to computers that are directly connected to the Internet (these are usually located in schools, businesses, government agencies, etc.). There are a number of types of domains on the Internet, and each has a specific designation which appears at the end of the e-mail addresses of its users. The most common domain types are:

DOMAIN	TYPE
.edu	Educational
.com	Commercial
.mil	Military
.gov	Governmental
.net	Internet resource
.org	Non-profit

When sending an e-mail message, it is very important to type the recipient's complete e-mail address with no errors. If there are mistakes in the address, the message will be returned with an error message indicating that the designated recipient is an unknown user and the message cannot be delivered.

In general, it does not matter whether e-mail addresses are typed in upper or lower case. It is advisable, however, that all e-mail addresses be typed exactly as they appear in the original source.

Using the Guide with E-Mail

An important e-mail address for you to remember is the one you can use for information about the *Guide* and the **Educational Psychology Home Page**: *edpsych@tmhe.com.* If you have any questions or comments, or experience any problems, send a message to this e-mail address. It was established in order to help users and to provide answers concerning the *Guide* and the **Home Page.**

Because of the significance of e-mail as a mode for many educators to reap the benefits of the Internet revolution, new information about productive e-mail addresses is provided regularly in the **What's New** section of the **Educational Psychology Home Page.**

Using E-Mail to Access Information

Using the Internet for e-mail allows users to send messages to and receive messages from each other at locations around the world at very low cost. Mail can be sent to multiple recipients, can be forwarded to other individuals, and can include additional materials as enclosures. A large amount of valuable information concerning educational resources can be obtained from the Internet through e-mail.

Throughout this *Guide*, useful Internet addresses are provided pertaining to educational psychology, learning, and teaching. In the *Guide*, we have attempted to include the best Internet sites in education — ones that are likely to be productive on a continuing basis. The majority of sites referenced can be reached directly through the menus on the **Educational Psychology Home Page**.

Educational Resources Information Center (ERIC)

Among the excellent Internet sites that can be accessed via e-mail are those associated with the Educational Resources Information Center (ERIC). ERIC is a nationwide information network maintained by the U.S. Department of Education which is designed to provide educators with ready access to education literature and resources. It is the largest education database in the world — containing more than 950,000 abstracts of journal articles, research reports, curriculum and teaching guides, conference papers, and books.

AskERIC is an e-mail-based question-and-answer service established specifically for educators to obtain information from ERIC. Anyone with a question about teaching and learning, educational administration or educational technology can get a response from AskERIC via e-mail. Its staff will provide an answer within approximately 48 hours. The response might include the full text of relevant ERIC Digests on education topics, a "mini-search" of the ERIC bibliographic database, and referrals to resource organizations. To use AskERIC:

1. Prepare your question as an e-mail message.
2. Request that information be sent to you on the topic.
3. Indicate the Subject: AskERIC <TOPIC>.
4. Send your message to the AskERIC Internet address: *askeric@ericir.syr.edu.*

ERIC has a toll-free phone number which can help you learn how to use its online system and can provide suggestions for making explorations of its components easy and successful. The number is 1-800-LET-ERIC. Additional information about the ERIC system can be obtained through most college and university libraries.

In addition to AskERIC, ERIC maintains many online services, including sixteen Subject Area Clearinghouses and several Adjunct Clearinghouses, all on education topics. These are also exceptional resources, providing a vast amount of information on central topics in education. Each of them is accessible via e-mail or through the AskERIC Virtual Library reached via either Gopher or the World Wide Web (see Parts 3 and 4 of the *Guide*).

E-mail addresses for fifteen Clearinghouses especially useful to teachers are:

ERIC SUBJECT AREA CLEARINGHOUSE	E-MAIL ADDRESS
Adjunct Test Collection Clearinghouse	*mhalpern@ets.org*
Adult, Career, and Vocational Education	*ericacve@magnus.acs.ohio-state.edu*
Assessment and Evaluation	*eric_ae@cua.edu*
Counseling and Student Services	*ericcass@dewey.uncg.edu*
Disabilities and Gifted Education	*ericec@cec.sped.org*
Elementary and Early Childhood Education	*ericeece@uiuc.edu*
ESL Literacy Education	*ncle@cal.org*
Information and Technology	*eric@ericir.syr.edu*
Language and Linguistics	*eric@cal.org*
Reading, English and Communication	*ericcs@ucs.indiana.edu*
Rural Education and Small Schools	*lanhamb@ael.org*
Science, Mathematics, Environmental Education	*ericse@osu.edu*
Social Studies/Social Science Education	*ericso@indiana.edu*
Teaching and Teacher Education	*ericsp@inet.ed.gov*
Urban Education	*eric-cue@columbia.edu*

You can use these e-mail addresses for seeking information from the ERIC Clearinghouses. Alternatively, you can search the contents on their Gopher and World Wide Web sites, accessible through the ERIC Databases listed on the **Educational Psychology Home Page**.

Using E-mail For Collaborative Online Learning Projects

E-mail can be used to obtain information from the Internet about thousands of other educational resources worldwide. Let us say, for example, an educational psychology class is interested in seeing examples of high quality instructional designs in online global learning projects for K-12 students. Many such projects exist and are being implemented involving children from several nations. The organizations sponsoring these sites and sources for finding out about them are identified throughout the *Guide*.

Academy One, for example, offers excellent telecomputing projects for K-12 students. It is part of the National Public Telecomputing Network (NPTN), a Free-Net organization which supports projects that charge no fee to participants. The *Academy One* projects show many applications of educational psychology in their instructional designs. They include examples of active problem solving and discovery learning and typically include collaborative projects among K-12 classes around the country.

The projects might include actual online discussions with members of Congressional Caucuses, in which students contribute their ideas. The projects might be national surveys of students on contemporary topics such as school violence, moral education and character development, or AIDS. The projects might involve K-12 students around the world comparing holidays and customs to discover similarities and differences. After participating in and analyzing results of collaborative activities, students brainstorm problem solutions. In order to obtain information about current and future projects:

1. Prepare an e-mail message requesting the information desired.
2. Specify the Subject: Academy One Projects.
3. Send the message to *info@nptn.org.*

A valuable source of information about collaborative learning projects and other resources on the Internet for K-12 teachers is *Best of K-12 Internet Resources,* available through Technology and Information Educational Services (TIES). This service provides an extensive compilation of K-12 educational information, including news, online guides, books, and access to other educational resource sites. The latter, accessible through keyword searches, leads to many other Internet sites relevant to K-12 education. TIES is owned and operated by eight greater-Minnesota school districts and 41 Twin Cities metropolitan area school districts. To obtain information from TIES:

1. Prepare an e-mail message requesting the information desired.
2. Indicate the Subject: Best of K-12 Internet Resources.
3. Send the message to *ties@ties.k12.mn.us.*

Discussion Groups: Listservs

People use the Internet to communicate with groups of individuals having interests like their own by way of mailing lists known as *listservs.* Also referred to as discussion lists, Internet listservs are typically focused on a particular topic. Listservs are automated mailing lists to which individuals can add their names (subscribe) via e-mail, after which they will start getting e-mail from that computer's mailing list and can begin posting messages. Individuals can remove their names (unsubscribe) via e-mail if they no longer want to receive e-mail from a particular listserv.

These discussion lists can be described using a number of comparisons. For students, they are in some ways like discussion sections, collaborative learning groups, or conversations — depending upon the nature of the list and the postings on it. The discussion lists can be helpful for obtaining up-to-date information, identifying a resource, locating a reference, networking with others on a campus or with K-12 teachers, or seeking partners to cooperate on a project.

There are two types of listservs — unmoderated and moderated. In each type, e-mail messages are sent by subscribers to the listserv's e-mail address, which then sends the message to all of the list subscribers. The difference is that in the case of unmoderated lists, which are found most frequently, messages are sent automatically. In the case of moderated lists, they are first reviewed by the listserv monitor.

You can become a member of most listservs easily and at no cost. There are many listservs that current and future teachers can participate in to enhance their understanding of teaching. Subscribing to them typically entails sending an e-mail message to the "subscription address" of the list. Leave the subject line of the message blank. In the body of the message, type

SUBSCRIBE LISTNAME <YOURFIRSTNAME YOURLASTNAME>. Examples focused on exploring uses of the Internet and electronic mail in K-12 classrooms are given below.

The Consortium for School Networking mailing list features discussions on collaborative learning projects for grades K-12, including many for elementary grade students. To subscribe:

1. Prepare e-mail that says in the message body: SUBSCRIBE COSNDISC <YOURFIRSTNAME YOURLASTNAME>.
2. Leave the Subject blank.
3. Send the message to the subscription address: *listproc@list.cren.net.*
4. Keep the return message, which will indicate the discussion address for sending e-mail to members of the list.

The highly active KIDSPHERE mailing list serves as an international computer network for K-12 children and teachers to discuss ongoing projects, school news, and other topics of interest. To subscribe:

1. Prepare e-mail that says in the message body: SUBSCRIBE KIDSPHERE <YOURFIRSTNAME YOURLASTNAME>.
2. Leave the Subject blank.
3. Send the message to the subscription address: *kidsphere-request@vms.cis.pitt.edu.*
4. Keep the return message, which will indicate the discussion address for sending e-mail to members of the list.

EDNET is a forum for exploring the educational potential of the Internet. To subscribe:

1. Prepare e-mail that says in the message body: SUBSCRIBE EDNET <YOURFIRSTNAME YOURLASTNAME>.
2. Leave the Subject blank.
3. Send the message to the subscription address: *listproc@lists.umass.edu.*
4. Keep the return message, which will indicate the discussion address for sending e-mail to members of the list.

Examples of other productive listservs in K-12 education are cited in other parts of the *Guide*. The three included on the next page are provided because they can help new teachers develop an understanding of educational issues that affect classroom practice.

LIST	LISTNAME	SUBSCRIPTION ADDRESS
AERA-Division C: Learning and Instruction	AERA-C	*listserv@asuvm.inre.asu.edu*
New and Improved Methods of Education	NEWEDU-L	*listserv@uhccvm.its.hawaii.edu*
Education Policy Analysis	EDPOLYAN	*listserv@asuvm.inre.asu.edu*

Listservs vary considerably in their volume of traffic. Once you have subscribed, you will receive all of the messages generated by the group until you unsubscribe. High-traffic lists can generate a dozen messages a day or more, so joining several of them will fill an e-mail mailbox rapidly and should be done with caution. If you no longer wish to subscribe to a list, you can easily unsubscribe. To do so:

1. Prepare e-mail having as a message body: UNSUBSCRIBE LISTNAME.
2. Leave the Subject blank.
3. Send the message to the subscription address you used to subscribe.

You can subscribe to a number of online newsletters through listservs. Three useful ones that are relevant to education, teaching and learning are described below, followed by their listserv addresses. For example, *Education Bulletin*, prepared by the Association for Supervision and Curriculum Development (ASCD), addresses current developments in education. It focuses on high-interest topics for educators in every subject, grade level, and interest area. Issued every two weeks, its articles include new ideas about working with today's students and about schools, curricula, and classrooms.

The subscription procedures are similar to those for other mailing lists, except your e-mail address goes in the message body:

1. Prepare an e-mail message that says in the message body: SUBSCRIBE BULLETIN <YOUR E-MAIL ADDRESS>.
2. Leave the Subject blank.
3. Send the message to the subscription address: *listserv@listserv.ascd.org*.

You might ask how you can become familiar with other online newsletters that are valuable K-12 resources. By becoming an active user of the Internet, you will find out about them from sources such as ERIC and *Classroom Connect*, a monthly periodical devoted to bringing the Internet into the K-12 classroom (e-mail: *connect@wentworth.com*). In addition, a number of Internet sites provide lists of education-related listservs. Some of these are included in "Additional Information Sources" on the **Internet Resources for Educators** menu discussed in Part 6.

"A relatively inexpensive technology, computer networking increasingly is being used in classrooms across the nation. Networks allow many students/teachers to communicate with many other students/teachers hence encouraging collaboration and active participation on the part of learners. Freeing learning from the constraint of geographic location, networks let learners and teachers participate in the education experience without regard to their physical location. Participants need not be constrained to traditional school-day hours and can take time in reviewing information presented on the network before responding, thus allowing for more thoughtful response.

Electronic communication can start when someone proposes an idea on the network. Others respond favorably to the idea, or the idea dies away. If there is favorable response, the interested individuals exchange electronic mail, and the idea's proponent sets up a conference."

Means, B., Blando, J., Olson, K., & Middleton, T. (1993). *Using technology to support education reform* (pp. 40-41). Newton, MA: Education Development Corporation.

part

3

Using Gopher Search and Retrieval to Access Internet Resources

Many resources located on the Internet are accessible through Gopher, a menu-based, search and retrieval system developed at the University of Minnesota in the early 1990's. It gives users a simple process through which to access locations where Internet text resources are stored. Gopher enables you to log onto a remote computer and download files available from it and other computers.

The Gopher system is an important place to look when exploring the Internet because, with its powerful search tools, it can be used rapidly and with very productive results. In many cases, sites have both Gopher and World Wide Web addresses. The difference is that at the Gopher site only textual information is available. Because some users may have access to Gopher but not the Web, several especially valuable education resources that are accessible both ways are described in this section.

Using Gopher

The Gopher search processes are interactive, branching either to broader subject categories or focusing in to narrow an original category. Because it provides access to extensive up-to-date and sophisticated textual information, Gopher is a useful resource for faculty and students using the Internet.

On Gopher, menus often lead to other menus, and these lead to additional menus. Items on it are primarily text files. Gopher is a well developed system, and most Internet service providers provide the tools for using it. TurboGopher is a very popular freestanding program for accessing and navigating the Gopher system over the Internet.

An especially valuable search tool for locating the extensive resources available on Gopher is Veronica (Very Easy Rodent-Oriented Netwide Index to Computerized Archives). Veronica makes possible the search of hundreds of thousands of Gopher menus (in "Gopherspace") available on the Internet for a specific topic. It enables the user to browse through and access material on an extensive variety of subjects simply by pointing and clicking.

Veronica maintains a database of all Gopher menu items at all Gopher servers that are known to it. It is, in essence, a database of databases composed of the complete set of Gopher sites. Veronica enables the user to search all of the known Gopher sites around the world for a specific topic.

In this Guide, several Gopher addresses are cited. They can be accessed either by using Veronica or, as will be done most frequently, using a Netscape (or another Web browser) as is discussed in Part 4. In this case, the address is preceded by the designation *gopher://*.

In exploring Gopher sites, users typically identify resources to which they want to return. For this purpose, Veronica has a system for saving *bookmarks* and entering them into one's own bookmark file — creating a personal annotated Gopher menu. When you find yourself in a valuable directory:

1. Click the pointer on Menu Items.
2. Select Bookmark from the menu.
3. The item will be saved in your bookmark file.
   Veronica will store your customized bookmark file for later use in the current Gopher session and in future sessions.

Valuable Resources Accessible Through Gopher

The **US. Department of Education** Gopher and Web sites provide a wide range of information valuable to educators and many links that make it a central site in finding and using education-related information on the Internet. Of special interest are the online *Teacher's Guide to the U.S. Department of Education* and *Researcher's Guide to the Department of Education*. Also of particular interest are the full texts of many reports and publications issued by the Department of Education. You will want to explore many links from the main menu or do a search on several keywords to find the array of materials that will be of interest to you. The Gopher address is *gopher://gopher.ed.gov*. (The Web address is *http://www.ed.gov*.)

ERIC's extensive bibliographic database of education-related literature, its Digests on important education topics, its collection of high quality lesson plans, and a variety of other resources are available through the AskERIC Virtual Library. The Gopher address is *gopher://ericir.syr.edu*. (The World Wide Web address, discussed in Part 4, is *http://ericir.syr.edu.)*

Daily Report Card is an online publication that provides updates on America's education reform efforts. It is a service of the Education Commission of the States and the National Education Goals Panel. Its Gopher address is *gopher://info.umd.edu*.

The National School Network Testbed has brought together schools around the nation in outstanding online projects. These have included Community of Explorers, InternNet, MicroMouse (Middle Schools), Urban Math collaboratives and Shadows (Elementary Schools). Its Gopher address is *gopher://copernicus.bbn.com/*. Its Web address is *http://nsn.bbn.com/*.

Guides to the Internet on the Catholic University Gopher contains information on many current and new Internet resources. One of its Internet Resource Guides, **Educational Resources Mailing List** (EDRES-L) provides reviews of education listserv discussion groups. Its database of Internet resources is located at its Gopher site: *gopher://gopher.cua.edu*.

The National Parent Information Network (NPIN), a national electronic network for parents, teachers, and others who work with parents and families, has a Gopher site maintained by the ERIC Clearinghouse on elementary and Early Childhood Education and the ERIC Clearinghouse on Urban Education. It includes publications relevant to parents, including (1) short articles on education topics, (2) listings of materials for parents from professional associations, and (3) descriptions of exemplary programs for parent education. *Resources for Those Who Work with Parents,* accessible at this Gopher site, can be extremely helpful in assisting parents to serve as the "first teacher" to their child and to support their child's learning throughout the school years. The Gopher address is *gopher://ericps.ed.uiuc.edu.* NPIN is also accessible on the World Wide Web, where its address is *http://ericps.ed.uiuc.edu/npin/npinhome.html.*

The **U.S. Library of Congress** is another vast resource available through Gopher that can be valuable to education students, particularly for class papers. The largest library in the world, it is reached via Gopher at *gopher://marvel.loc.gov/.*

These are only a few examples of the resources that are available to you through Gopher sites on the Internet. It is important to note that Gopher sites can now be accessed on the World Wide Web. This is done by using *gopher://* followed by the site's Gopher address. Especially valuable Gopher sites for educators have been included on the **Educational Psychology Home Page**. Additional sites are added regularly and described in the **What's New** section of the **Home Page**.

References

Houston, J. (Ed.). (1995). *Thesaurus of ERIC Descriptors* (13th ed.). Phoenix, AZ: Oryx Press.

Rothenberg, D. (1995). *The Internet and early childhood educators: Some frequently asked questions.* Urbana, IL: ERIC Clearinghouse on Elementary and Early Childhood Education, University of Illinois.

Smarte, L. (1995). *All about ERIC.* Washington, DC: Educational Resources Information Center, National Library of Education, Office of Educational Research and Improvement, U.S. Department of Education.

part

4

The World Wide Web and Its Extensive Capabilities

A vast array of resources are available on the World Wide Web (alternately referred to as "WWW" or simply "the Web"), a revolutionary interconnection of information sites located on "Home Pages" which incorporate text, graphics, video, and sound. The Web is a spiderweb-like interconnection of millions of information resources located on computers worldwide. It offers easy, attractive access to a vast number of sites. Users click on "links" (usually buttons or underlined text) which take them immediately to other sites on computers anywhere in the world containing more information about the topic.

A WWW Home Page typically includes a brief introduction to the Home Page, graphics, and instructions on using the Home Page to access additional information. WWW Home Pages usually include a set of links and pointers that guide individuals to resources throughout the Internet and World Wide Web.

User-Friendly Tools for Exploring the Web

Netscape is currently the most frequently used Web browser or navigation tool. It is software that allows users to access and navigate the Web through graphical point-and-click interfaces. While exploring the Web, users will typically identify resources to which they want to return. For this purpose, Netscape has a simple procedure enabling users to save bookmarks and enter them into their own bookmark file — their personal annotated Web menu (similar to that described in Part 3 for Gopher sites on Veronica).

Users can explore the extensive resources of the Internet and the World Wide Web with little or no assistance. They can identify and create bookmarks for materials and sites relevant to their study of a field such as education. In order to develop a "sense" of how to explore Web sites efficiently, they will need to begin by selecting one of the most frequently used *Web search engines.* These are Web-searching tools which have been indexed by subject. They allow individuals to do searches on specific topics in hundreds of fields such as education through keyword searches.

The most frequently used Web search engines include *Alta Vista, Excite, InfoSeek, Lycos, Open Text, WebCrawler* and *Yahoo*. These search engines typically include Gopher sites as well as Web sites in its searches. The Web addresses (Uniform Resource Locators — URLs) for these frequently used search engines are given below. However, you can access them all directly and immediately on the **Educational Psychology Home Page**. They are located on the menu accessed by clicking on **Tools for Exploring the Internet**.

WEB SEARCH ENGINE	WEB ADDRESS
Alta Vista	*http://altavista.digital.com/*
Excite	*http://www.excite.com/*
InfoSeek	*http://www.infoseek.com/*
Lycos	*http://www.lycos.com/*
Open Text	*http://index.opentext.net/*
WebCrawler	*http://webcrawler.com/*
Yahoo	*http://www.yahoo.com/*

After a bit of experience, it will become easier for you to make sense of Web addresses. The "http" at the beginning refers to Hypertext Transport Protocol. This is the computer language that Web sites and Web browsers use to transmit information to and from each other. The "html" at the end refers to Hypertext Markup Language, the programming language of the Web that is used to turn a document into a World Wide Web page.

After activating a search engine such as the popular ones listed above, you are asked to enter the keyword(s) on which you want a search conducted. Immediately, the search engine identifies materials on the Web that relate to the keyword. You can typically specify the number of items you wish to view. It is often valuable to limit the number initially to 10 or 20 items to ensure that the keyword(s) you entered have yielded a productive search. You can then specify as many items as you want to view or, potentially, designate a different keyword that may yield a more successful search.

For example, you might enter the keywords *Education, Education (K-12)* or *Educational Psychology.* A few seconds after Enter or Return is pressed, a list of sites will be provided on the screen. You then select the first site to be explored, and the search engine takes you there. After you select, read (and, if desired, print) the items of interest, you click on the button indicating "Back" (which typically is in a box at the top left of the screen). You then return to the list of sites identified for you. You repeat this process of selecting and examining for each of the sites identified by the search engine that you want to explore.

It is important to understand that information on the Internet is unrestricted, and that this has benefits and drawbacks in terms of its serving as an instructional resource. This *Guide* and the **Educational Psychology Home Page** are designed in part to compensate for one of the problems in using the Internet as an instructional resource: many sites contain materials that are not of sufficient quality to be useful for a particular instructional purpose. In addition, general search engines, even when searching for carefully designated keywords, typically do not differentiate beyond titles in determining relevance. Hence, an individual may spend four or five hours and identify only a handful of high quality, relevant resources. It can be difficult to locate highly valuable resources. If you do not know what sites tend to be especially productive, you may miss some of the best information, materials and databases while spending time exploring relatively unproductive sites. The concept of the *Guide* and the **Home Page** is to help you locate the most valuable sites and, in addition, to give you the tools to explore the Internet more broadly.

Examples of Valuable Resources on the Web

Hundreds of Web sites have been created that are valuable resources for educators. You will want to know how you can become and stay informed of these outstanding sites. First, begin using the Web and explore the sites identified in the *Guide*. Experiment with the common Web search engines, which have links to valuable resources and to relatively unproductive sites as well. The Site Index and General References at the end of the *Guide* will help you identify productive sites. However, because the Web is changing constantly, you need a more dynamic process for staying up-to-date on current and outstanding sites. Good procedures include joining listservs, exploring the AskERIC Virtual Library, and browsing newsgroup postings on a periodic basis. They will have information about new and current Web sites that are especially valuable.

Accessing the AskERIC Virtual Library

The AskERIC Virtual Library is directly accessible through the **Educational Psychology Home Page**. To explore it from the **Home Page**:

1. Click on **Internet Resources for Educators.**
2. Select ERIC and click on it.
3. Choose the item on the ERIC menu you wish to explore and click on it.
4. Most items on ERIC can be printed out easily. When you wish to make a copy of an item, click the Print box at the top of the ERIC screen or use the usual print command for your computer.
5. If you wish to explore another ERIC menu item, click on Back at the top left of the screen.
6. This will take you to the previous ERIC menus, from which you can select another item to explore.
7. Repeat the procedure as necessary to explore each item of interest to you on the ERIC menu.

A good place to begin using the AskERIC Virtual Library is the link *About AskERIC*. It will give you information about the system that will help you explore it further.

1. Select *About AskERIC* by clicking on it.
   The next screen will be Greetings and Welcome to the AskERIC Service for Educators.
2. Read the basic information about the ERIC system.
3. Click Back in the top left of the screen to return to the previous screens and return to the Main Menu.

Among the extremely valuable resources available in the AskERIC Virtual Library is the ERIC Resources file which contains the ERIC Digests. The ERIC Digests are hundreds of outstanding summaries of "the knowledge base" related to topics in education. These short overviews typically integrate theory, research and educational practice on central topics in education.

Another exceptionally valuable resource is the ERIC Bibliographic Database. It includes bibliographic information and abstracts for hundreds of thousands of educational documents, including books, journal articles, research studies, and conference papers. It was created by the U.S. Department of Education to serve as the National Library of Education.

The ERIC Bibliographic Database (referred to as the ERIC Database) is one of the many valuable ERIC menu items for faculty and students. Containing more than 950,000 documents, it is the world's largest source of education information. It is created from: (a) *Resources in Education* (RIE), a database of conference papers, research reports, unpublished manuscripts, books, and technical reports; and (b) *Current Index to Journals in Education* (CIJE), a database of journal articles that covers periodical literature. ERIC contains articles from more than 800 education-related journals.

Searches of the ERIC Bibliographic Database are conducted using keywords that reflect the topic of interest (searches are also frequently conducted by author name). The indexing source used for accessing information is an extensive list of subject headings, called *Descriptors,* contained in the *Thesaurus of ERIC Descriptors,* which is available at most college or university libraries. You can conduct a search of the ERIC Bibliographic Database by any keyword in the ERIC Thesaurus or by an author's name or by a title. After you enter the search word or words, you are asked for the number of documents you want to have displayed. ERIC then conducts a search and sends the abstracts located to your computer.

You get an online "report" which tells you the number of "finds" and the number of "displayed" items from the search. The report is an annotated bibliography containing the abstracts of the research and publications found through your search, typically materials dated within the past five years — although you can request earlier materials.

The Thesaurus of ERIC Descriptors uses common terminology in the field of education, and most users can conduct searches successfully trying variations of the terms that are used in the particular field of study. Many of the key terms in textbooks are generally in the ERIC Thesaurus and can be used successfully as search words. For help finding the appropriate Descriptor to use as a search word, you can call the ERIC help line at 1-800-LET ERIC.

For each item displayed from the ERIC Bibliographic Database, several valuable types of information are provided. These include:

ERIC Document Number
Author(s)
Title
Date Published
Descriptive Note (Pages)
ERIC Document Reproduction Service (EDRS) Availability
Publication Type (Research Report, Book, etc.)
Descriptors (from the ERIC Thesaurus)
Abstract

The ERIC Document Number enables you to access publications listed in the ERIC system. This number can be used to obtain the complete document for most items from either (a) a college/university library microfiche collection or (b) the ERIC Document Reproduction Service (EDRS), which provides FAX order and delivery service if requested (Phone: 800/443-ERIC; FAX: 703/440-1408).

The AskERIC Virtual Library contains more than 1,000 lesson plans organized by subject and grade level. They are accessed by selecting AskERIC Lesson Plans. The resulting menu enables you to search for lesson plans by subject and includes, in addition, new lesson plans added on a frequent basis.

Another useful resource is the set of ERIC Bibliographies located under ERIC Resources. These are comprehensive annotated bibliographies of articles on selected timely and important topics. Examples include: *Cooperative Learning; Disabled Students in Mainstreamed Classes: Supporting Inclusion, Fostering Success; Infusing Multicultural Education Into Today's Schools;* and *Providing "Hands-On" Learning Experiences to Support Traditional Learning Objectives.*

ERIC is, in addition, an excellent source for obtaining information on productive education listservs. Its online Education Listserv Archives includes a selected menu of high quality listservs. The Archives include messages posted on the listservs for the past several months.

ERIC also provides an online calendar of education conferences. Additionally, it lists news and announcements of professional organizations. Among other resource materials are its list of electronic journals, books, and reference tools and its Internet Guides and Directories, which provide information about the Internet and what can be found on it.

All of the major components of **ERIC** can be accessed easily using the World Wide Web. The Web address for the **AskERIC Virtual Library** is

http://ericir.syr.edu. The Web site (like the Gopher site) enables you to access the key ERIC databases: (a) the Bibliographic Database; (b) the ERIC Digests; (c) lesson plans by subject and grade level; and (d) information about professional organizations, conferences, and listservs. ERIC's Subject Area Educational Clearinghouses, which contain detailed information on their respective topics, can also be accessed through the AskERIC Virtual Library Web site (and the Gopher site).

Some Examples of Additional Web Sites

The **U.S. Department of Education** Web Site is another extremely valuable resource for educators which, like the AskERIC Virtual Library, contains much of the same information as its Gopher site. It has separate links to hundreds of education resources ranging from materials concerning the National Education Goals to reports issued by the U.S. Department of Education. The numerous significant reports available on it include ones addressing effective instructional strategies in the various subject areas, parent and family involvement in education, and approaches for making better use of and extending the time students spend in learning.

The U.S. Department of Education Web site also includes information about federal programs for early childhood, elementary, secondary and postsecondary education. It also has links to major federally supported

National Research and Development Centers and the Regional Educational Laboratories, which contain online materials on all aspects of K-12 education. The Web address for the U.S. Department of Education Home Page is *http://www.ed.gov.*

FedWorld, the U.S. government's Home Page on the World Wide Web, has links to more than 1,000 databases maintained by various government agencies and departments. Many of these contain outstanding resource materials (e.g., Declaration of Independence, Emancipation Proclamation, NASA Space Shuttle Images, Census Data) that can be used in K-12 classrooms. Its World Wide Web address is *http://www.fedworld.gov.*

The **White House** has created its own Web page. On it can be found messages from the President and Vice President and many resources related to the government's interest in advancing national and international uses of technology and telecommunications. The Web address is *http://www. whitehouse.gov/WH/Welcome.html.*

Thomas is a Web site established by the U.S. Congress. It lets you search both proposed and passed legislation of both the current and last sessions of Congress. An initial search will show the names of all bills containing whatever keyword you type in. Select a bill and you can read its text. You can also search the *Congressional Record* in the same way. This resource enables you to obtain federal legislation and to find out what Congressional leaders are saying about key education topics. Its Web address is *http://thomas.loc.gov.*

Classroom Connect is the largest newsletter in the country focused on using the Internet in K-12 classrooms. Its weekly newsletter, which helps educators to identify and explore Internet resources and identifies new K-12 sites, materials and projects on the Internet, is circulated through fee-based subscriptions. However, materials from it — new educational links, lesson plan suggestions, and full-length articles from the *Classroom Connect* newsletter — are posted each week on the Web site. The site also contains Classroom Web, a collection of Web pages created by K-12 schools. Its address is *http://www. wentworth.com/.*

The **National Center for Supercomputing Applications (NCSA)** has organized a Web site to show students and teachers how they can connect with and use educational resources on the Internet. On its Web page, one finds Internet tutorials and a variety of valuable links for K-12 educators. Its address is *http://www.ncsa.uiuc.edu/Edu/ EduHome.html.*

The **Urban Education Web** is the site of the ERIC Clearinghouse on Urban Education and is maintained by Teachers College at Columbia University. It contains a comprehensive set of resources, studies and reports related to fostering success among students in urban areas. Its address is *http://eric-web.tc.columbia.edu/.*

These are only a few examples of the hundreds of Web sites that are valuable resources for current and future educators. Their easy accessibility has profound implications for educational psychology. The attributes of the Web allow for a transformation in the nature of learning and teaching. Rather than simply acquiring information and knowledge, students can actively participate — with their peers and teachers — in collaborative discovery, analysis, and communication on the frontiers of knowledge.

part

5

Educational Psychology Home Page: An Overview

The **Educational Psychology Home Page** enables you to locate on the Internet thousands of resources relevant to the study of education and to becoming an educator who is well prepared for the 21st century. The **Educational Psychology Home Page** and its linked series of topic-oriented Web pages are designed to empower you to learn through your own active exploration of areas that are of interest to you. They are structured to introduce you to hundreds of sites on the Internet where you can locate overviews of key concepts, research abstracts, discussion groups, instructional materials and projects which you will be able to share with your own students.

Learning to Use the Educational Psychology Home Page

Before you begin exploring the **Educational Psychology Home Page**, it is valuable to consider your own sense of self-efficacy in relation to technology. Self-efficacy is "people's judgments of their capabilities to organize and execute courses of action to gain designated types of performances" (Bandura, 1986). An efficacy expectation is "an individual's belief that he or she can perform the behavior or behaviors required to produce certain outcomes" (Elliott et al., 1996, p. 351).

There is an important relationship between self-efficacy, motivation, and success among learners (Crowl et al., 1997). Research indicates that "the student who asks questions and obtains assistance when it is required alleviates immediate learning difficulties and also acquires knowledge and skills which can be used for self-help later" (Newman, 1990). There is considerable literature demonstrating the value of cooperative learning, where students help one another approach new tasks (Slavin, 1988).

As you begin planning your use of the Internet, you may experience obstacles to your own learning that relate to your sense of efficacy. If you have not previously used the Internet, you are likely to have fears about the difficulties that lie ahead. No matter what your fears, once you move beyond them you will find using the Internet very easy. The simple fact is that using the Internet is likely to be one of the easiest things you have mastered in years. Recognize that once you start using it, you will immediately begin experiencing success and the world will be, literally, at your fingertips. If you need help, ask questions of those around you. Select a peer to explore with you so that you can help one another learn. As you make rapid progress, consider the implications for helping your own students when fears interfere with learning.

Getting to Know the Educational Psychology Home Page

Begin exploring the **Educational Psychology Home Page** by activating Netscape or another Web browser used by your Internet service provider and connecting to the **Home Page.** The set of steps involved in getting to the **Educational Psychology Home Page** are described below.

1. Activate your connection to the Internet (e.g., through your campus computer center, America Online, etc.).
2. Open Netscape or whatever WWW navigation tool is used by your provider.
3. In the "Netsite" or "Location" dialogue box at the top of the screen, type the address of the **Educational Psychology Home Page**:

   http://www.bbp.com/edpsych.html

4. Press Return or Enter.

This takes you immediately to the **Educational Psychology Home Page** and marks your successful navigation on the World Wide Web. When you connect with the **Educational Psychology Home Page**, you will find a screen that shows five underlined subject areas. Each is a link that can be clicked on to proceed to the specific **Web Page** that contains information related to that subject area.

Components of the Home Page

The five subject area links contained on the **Home Page** are described below.

Tools for Exploring the Internet

This link takes you to a Web page that contains the most popular search engines for exploring the Internet. By selecting one and clicking on it, you will be able to begin exploring the Internet. The search engines include:

Alta Vista
Excite
InfoSeek
Lycos
Open Text
WebCrawler
Yahoo

What's New

This link takes you to a Web page which contains concise updates on news and research related to education, teaching and learning. It also identifies new materials on the Internet, the Web, and the **Educational Psychology Web Pages. What's New** will help you integrate current happenings in K-12 education, new resources on the Internet, and your study of educational psychology.

Internet Resources for Educators

This link takes you to a Web page that lists resources containing such items as: Databases & Informational Resources (ERIC Digests, ERIC Bibliographic Database, etc.); Instructional Resources (Lesson Plans, Learning Projects, Instructional Materials); Online Journals; Educational Associations & Organizations; and Additional Information Sources.

Educational Psychology Topics

This link takes you to a Web page containing descriptions of Internet resources organized by primary topics in *Educational Psychology: Windows on Teaching* and *Educational Psychology: Effective Teaching, Effective Learning*. These topics are also found in most other basic and advanced educational psychology texts.

Communications and General Interest Topics

This link takes you to a Web page related to (a) communications, including a list of listservs, and (b) sources of information about Educational Conferences, Education Grants, and Job Searches.

<u>References</u>

Bandura, A. (1986). *Social foundations of thought and action: A social-cognitive theory.* Englewood Cliffs, NJ: Prentice Hall.

Crowl, T., Kaminsky, S. and Podell, D.M. (1997). *Educational psychology: Windows on teaching.* Dubuque, IA: Times Mirror Higher Education Group.

Elliott, S., Kratochwill, T., Littlefield, J., & Travers, J. (1996). *Educational psychology: Effective teaching, effective learning* (2nd ed.). Dubuque, IA: Times Mirror Higher Education Group.

Newman, R.S. (1990). Children's help-seeking in the classroom: The role of motivational factors and attitudes. *Journal of Educational Psychology, 82,* 71-80.

Slavin, R. (1988). Synthesis of research on grouping in elementary and secondary schools. *Educational Leadership, 64,* (1), 67-77.

part

6

Educational Psychology Home Page: Internet Resources for Educators

This part of the *Guide* provides an overview of some of the Internet and World Wide Web resources accessible through the **Educational Psychology Web Page** entitled **Internet Resources for Educators**. Clicking on the associated link on the **Home Page** takes you to this page, where you will find the following menu:

Databases and Informational Resources

A vast number of databases and informational resources are accessible through the Internet, but only a limited number are large and of high quality in the field of education. Examples of some particularly valuable ones are identified below. Internet sites that are included in **Additional Information Sources** augment these listings.

The Internet databases most directly relevant to K-12 teaching and learning are those of **ERIC** *(http://ericir.syr.edu/Eric/)* and the **AskERIC Virtual Library** *(http://ericir.syr.edu)*. The contents of these exceptionally valuable and comprehensive databases were described briefly in parts 3 and 4 of the *Guide*. Additional databases accessible through the ERIC system include the Test Locator Database, the Test Review Locator Database, and the Educational Testing Service (ETS) Test Collection.

Other large informational resources on the Internet addressing a broad set of topics useful to educators include the **U.S. Department of Education** (*http://www.ed.gov*) and **FedWorld** (*http://www.fedworld.gov*). From the U.S. Department of Education Home Page, you can access the federally sponsored National Research Centers and Regional Educational Laboratories and the ERIC Subject Area Clearinghouses, all of which contain additional valuable resources.

Instructional Resources

Instructional Resources is another item on the **Internet Resources for Educators** Web page. Under it, three types of instructional resources are listed: *Lesson Plans, Learning Projects*, and *Instructional Materials*. By clicking on a specific resource listed below each one of them, you will have access to Internet sites that contain information relevant to that topic.

Lesson Plans

Lesson Plans that represent excellent instructional resources and that have been catalogued by a number of different organizations are included on the **Internet Resources for Educators** Web page under *Lesson Plans*. Examples, including the sources of the lesson plans and their Internet addresses, are given below.

SOURCE OF LESSON PLAN	INTERNET ADDRESS
Classroom Connect	*http://www.wentworth.com/*
Environmental Education Link (EE-LINK)	*http://www.nceet.snre.umich.edu*
ERIC	*http://ericir.syr.edu/Virtual/Lessons/*
KIDLINK	*http://www.kidlink.org/*
K-12 Sources, Curriculum, Lesson Plans	*http://execpc.com:80/~dboals/k-12.html*
National School Network Testbed	*http://nsn.bbn.com/*

Learning Projects

The **Internet Resources for Educators** Web page also includes *Learning Projects*. This section provides a list of exemplary learning projects on the Web. Like the other materials on the **Educational Psychology Web Pages**, this is not an exhaustive list but rather a set illustrative of high quality learning projects. Many of the learning projects focus on online learning experiences for students in grades K-12. They cover every K-12 subject, and some are international in scope. They have been chosen because they demonstrate attributes of (a) effective instructional design and (b) using technology to change teaching and learning experiences in substantial ways.

Typically, they illustrate a mode of instruction in which teachers serve as facilitators and students are engaged in authentic, challenging tasks. The projects are multidisciplinary, occur over extended blocks of time, and enable students to explore and to use advanced skills (Means et al., 1993).

Often, students are involved in working with real data, in collaborative learning, in questioning, analyzing and discussing what they have learned. They are able to experience geographically distant phenomena and different cultures. In a number of cases, the projects enable students to appreciate the value of other languages for communicating with students elsewhere. In most, their learning relates to the real world and helps them answer questions that are meaningful to them.

Other projects include a substantial writing component. Thinking and composition skills take on considerable importance to the students because they are used in activities that are meaningful to them and that entail communicating with other students elsewhere (Means et al., 1993).

Examples of sources of learning projects and their Internet locations are given below. You can go to each directly by selecting it from the *Learning Projects* menu on the **Internet Resources for Educators** Web page.

LEARNING PROJECTS	INTERNET ADDRESS
Academy One	*http://www.nptn.org/cyber.serv/AOneP/*
Educational Projects Online	*http://pixel.cs.vt.edu/melissa/projects.html*
Global SchoolNet Foundation	*http://gsn.org/*
NASA K-12 Projects	*http://quest.arc.nasa.gov*
National School Network Testbed	*http://nsn.bbn.com/*
TERC/The Hub for Mathematics and Science Education Reform	*http://hub.terc.edu*
Whole Frog Project	*http://george.lbl.gov/*

Instructional Materials

A large array of materials valuable for teaching can be found on the World Wide Web. These can be particularly useful as educators develop instructional strategies and lesson plans responsive to the strengths, needs and differences among individual learners in their classrooms. Examples of some excellent online resources applicable to a variety of subject areas are listed below. They are among the resources directly accessible on the *Instructional Materials* menu on the **Internet Resources for Educators** Web page.

INSTRUCTIONAL MATERIALS	INTERNET ADDRESS
Britannica Online	*http://www.eb.com/*
Exploratorium	*http://www.exploratorium.edu*
Library Without Walls	*gopher://dewey.lib.ncsu.edu/*
STEIS (Space Telescope Electronic Information System)	*http://www.stsci.edu//*
Weather, Current – U.S.	*http://www.mit.edu:8001/usa.html*
Weather, Current – Maps/Movies	*http://rs560.cl.msu.edu/weather/*

Online Journals

Online Journals provides access to education journals and newsletters that are available directly on the Internet. This resource includes online publications and directories having particular relevance to educational psychology. Included are:

RESOURCE	INTERNET ADDRESS
Directory of Online Journals (CICNet)	*gopher://gopher.cic.net:2000/11/e-serials*
Education Policy Analysis Archives	*http://seamonkey.ed.asu.edu/epaa/*
Educational Research Newsletter	*http://www.capecod.net/ern/ern_home.html*
inQuiry Almanac	*http://sln.fi.edu/qanda/qanda.html*
Learning Research and Development Center *Newsletter*	*gopher://gopher.pitt.edu*

Educational Associations and Organizations

This section contains Web addresses for a number of educational organizations and associations. Most of the sites have links to other Web locations relevant to their emphases.

ASSOCIATION/ORGANIZATION	INTERNET ADDRESS
National Council of Teachers of English	*http://www.ncte.org/*
National Council of Teachers of Mathematics (NCTM) Standards	*http://www.emich.edu/public/nasa/mathemat.htm*
National Science Teachers Association	*http://www.nsta.org/*
National Council for the Social Studies (NCSS) Online	*http://www.ncss.org/online/*

Additional Information Sources

There are hundreds of additional information sources on the Internet that provide high quality resources in the field of education. Some of these relate to theories and research on teaching and learning. Others provide examples and resources for applying the concepts that are most fundamental within educational psychology. They facilitate, for example, the preparation of instruction that matches the developmental level of each student, that is intrinsically motivating, and that enables students to work cooperatively in productive and collaborative learning groups.

The **Additional Information Sources** have been carefully selected to represent high quality Internet sites that will be useful to most individuals pursuing careers in education. A number of examples follow.

Education: On-Line Teaching and Learning (Yahoo) contains a comprehensive set of resources for using technology in the classroom. Its Web address is *http://www.yahoo.com/Education/On_line_Teaching_and_Learning/.*

K-12 Sources, Curriculum, Lesson Plans links to hundreds of productive Internet sites containing useful education resources. It also contains a menu of high quality lessons. Its Web address is *http://execpc.com:80/~dboals/k-12.html.*

Pathways to School Improvement is on the Web site maintained by the North Central Regional Educational Laboratory, sponsored by the U.S. Department of Education. Its menu includes links to many excellent educational documents, on-line resources, and K-12 Internet projects and contains an outstanding series of papers on *Critical Issues* related to school improvement. Its Web address is *http://www.ncrel.org/.*

The Hub for Mathematics and Science Education Reform provides articles, curriculum and project reports on mathematics, science and technology education reform. It is maintained by TERC in conjunction with a Regional Alliance of K-12 educators, higher education faculty, and mathematics and science education specialists and is supported by the U.S. Department of Education. Its Web address is *http://hub.terc.edu*

Teachers Helping Teachers is a Web site addressing many topics of central interest to teachers. Its address is *http://www.pacificnet.net/~mandel/.*

The **University of California at Irvine Department of Education** has established a Home Page that contains links to many valuable sites for educators on the Internet. Its Web address is *http://www.gse.uci.edu.*

Examples of other valuable Web sites contained on the **Additional Information Sources** menu are listed on the next page.

ADDITIONAL INFORMATION SOURCES	INTERNET ADDRESS
Association for Supervision and Classroom Development (ASCD)	*http://www.ascd.org*
Classroom Connect	*http://www.wentworth.com*
Committee on Institutional Cooperation (CICNet)	*gopher://gopher.cic.net*
Consortium for School Networking	*http://cosn.org*
Daily Report Card	*gopher://info.umd.edu/*
Guides to the Internet	*gopher://gopher.cua.edu:70/11/internet-tools*
Eisenhower National Clearinghouse for Mathematics and Science Education	*http://www.enc.org*
Frank Potter's Science Gems	*http://www-sci.lib.uci.edu/SEP/SEP.html*
K-12 Super Index	*http://www.lloyd.com*
National Center for Research on Evaluation, Standards, and Student Testing	*http://www.cse.ucla.edu*
National Center for Supercomputing Applications	*http://www.ncsa.uiuc.edu/Edu/EduHome.html*
National Parent Information Network	*http://ericps.ed.uiuc.edu/npin/*
National Science Foundation	*http://www.nsf.gov/*
Online Discussion Groups (listservs) and Electronic Journals	*http://k12.cnidr.org:90/lists.html*
Technology and Information Educational Services (TIES) – Minnesota	*http://tiesnet.ties.k12.mn.us*
Thomas	*http://thomas.loc.gov*
Urban Education Web	*http://eric-web.tc.columbia.edu/*
U.S. Library of Congress	*gopher://marvel.loc.gov/*
White House	*http://www.whitehouse.gov*
World Wide Web Virtual Library Museum Page	*http://palimpsest.stanford.edu/icom/vlmp/*

References

Means, B., Blando, J., Olson, K., & Middleton, T. (1993). *Using technology to support education reform.* Newton, MA: Education Development Center.

part

7

Educational Psychology Home Page: Communications and General Interest Topics

The **Educational Psychology Home Page** includes a link to **Communications and General Interest Topics.** This Web page provides a menu designed specifically to be responsive to the interests of students and faculty in educational psychology and related education classes. Its menu items are as follow:

Communications
Education Conferences
Education Grants
Job Search

Communications

Communications is a continuously evolving component of the **Educational Psychology Home Page** One of its features is a list of links to sources of information. A second feature is a list of listservs in which participants share messages related to common areas of interest. These listservs provide the opportunity for education students and faculty to read messages from and post messages to individuals in the field of education having interests similar to their own. They provide a unique opportunity for current and future professionals in the field of education to see a wide range of perspectives on a wide-ranging group of topics. Each listserv can be subscribed to using the procedures described in Part 2 under *Electronic Mail*.

Additional Communications components are intended to reflect input and feedback from students and faculty using the **Educational Psychology Web Pages**. Examples of potential items include student and faculty exchanges related to educational psychology course work and collaborative projects for classes and students in education.

Bulletin Board Systems

Bulletin board systems (BBSs) can be small, local dial-up services available by modem — or larger systems that exist on the Internet. They serve as forums for users to browse and exchange text information and files. They are typically free, and the thousands that have been created by educators are often a rich source of lesson plans and of exchanges among schools in local areas. Some local BBSs provide access to the Internet and Internet newsgroups.

The *Global SchoolNet Foundation* is a unique resource that can help you (a) identify providers of free e-mail accounts on the Internet and (b) locate and participate in bulletin boards focused on K-12 education. It will enable you to select from hundreds of electronic bulletin boards around the world. Each bulletin board represents a "node" on the Global SchoolNet system, which many teachers and students use for e-mail. The nodes are located at such places as school districts, county or regional education agencies, local schools, and colleges and universities.

A particular focus of Global SchoolNet is offering curriculum-based online learning projects in which any classroom can participate. For educational psychology classes, these are excellent resources for examining educational objectives and the design and assessment of classroom instructional activities. The Global SchoolNet Foundation is listed in the **Communications** menu on the **Communications and General Interest Topics** Web page. Its Web address is *http://gsn.org/*.

Another resource for identifying local, national and international bulletin boards is K12Net. It refers to itself as a "network with training wheels" that provides schools with an introduction to the world of international telecommunications. It consists of hundreds of locally owned and operated school-based electronic bulletin board systems throughout the world that are all networked to each other and to other networks. It is a subset of FidoNet, which connects over 25,000 locally owned and operated BBSs worldwide. They are all open to use without charge (except for the cost of the local phone calls). Over 10,000 of them are in the U.S. There is a FidoNet BBS in virtually every small and large city in the U.S., as well as in large numbers of rural locations.

K12Net is the K-12 educational portion of FidoNet. K12Net is designed specifically for elementary and secondary teachers, and nearly twenty percent of the ongoing "conversations" are between teachers all over the world. They share ideas on teaching strategies, curricula, and instructional materials in their particular subject areas. K12Net is listed on the **Communications** menu. Its Web address is *http://www.vivanet.com/freenet/k/K12Net/*.

It is important to point out here that the Global SchoolNet Foundation (and K12Net) facilitates telecommunications among local bulletin board users. A computer, modem, and telephone connection to a local bulletin board via communications software are all that are needed to participate in them.

Many of the bulletin board systems provide the communications software when you sign up. If not, some of the best programs (Z-Term, FreeTerm, etc.) are available as freeware or shareware.

Primary objectives of both the Global SchoolNet Foundation and K12Net include enabling educators to participate in the global community of international telecommunications through no more than a local phone call from a user's modem.

Even if you do not have access to the Internet, you can nevertheless participate in electronic communication and information exchange. If you need to locate a local bulletin board, either the Global SchoolNet Foundation or K12Net can help you do so.

Education Conferences

There are a number of Internet sites that provide information about conferences in the field of education. Two examples are **AskERIC Virtual Library** (*Education Conferences — Calendars and Announcements*) and **K-12 Sources, Curriculum, Lesson Plans** (*Conferences, Organizations and Publications*). ***Classroom Connect*** provides information about conferences addressing the use of the Internet in K-12 education and related topics. **Education Conferences** on the **Communications and General Interest Topics** Web page provides a menu of links to sources of information such as these.

Many bulletin boards and newsgroups post information about conferences in their geographic and subject matter areas. Going to them directly will enable you to find out more about localized and specialized conference information. Part 2 of the *Guide* describes procedures for accessing them.

Education Grants

Numerous resources exist on the Web for locating federal, state, corporate, and foundation (philanthropic) grants for K-12 education. These include grants for schools and school district projects, for research, and for innovation on the part of individual teachers or groups of teachers. The sites described below will provide a substantial amount of information and will help you identify additional sources of grant information in areas of particular interest to you. All are accessible on the **Education Grants** menu of the **Communications and General Interest Topics** Web Page.

Grants Information Gophers is a useful resource that links you with information regarding education grants and funding, as well as online guides to funding sources. Its Gopher address is *gopher://k12.oit.umass.edu:70/11/grants/grants*.

The **GrantsWeb** is another helpful resource that provides information on the U.S. Department of Education, the Foundation Center, the National Science Foundation, and other nationwide grant programs. Its Web address is *http://infoserv.rttonet.psu.edu/gweb.htm*.

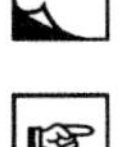

The **U.S. Department of Education** Web site provides information concerning grants, contracts, and fellowships that are available through a broad range of federal education programs. The information is in the Department's Web site at *Money Matters*. The Web site address is *http://www.ed.gov*.

The **Eisenhower National Clearinghouse for Mathematics and Science Education** provides online grant information and links to other sites that describe grant resources. The Web address is *http://www.enc.org*.

The **Research Services Gopher** provides connections to comprehensive databases of grants from federal agencies. It provides online access to the

Catalogue of Federal Domestic Assistance (CFDA), which contains a listing of all federal grants. The Research Service's Gopher address is *gopher://solar.rtd.utk.edu.*

Another source of information about grants for education and of resources in technology and other areas is the **Far West Educational Laboratory,** supported in part by the U.S. Department of Education. Its Web address is *http://www.fwl.org.*

Job Search

A number of Internet sites provide useful information about preparing resumes, conducting job searches, and identifying job opportunities. Sites that are included on the **Job Search** menu on the **Communications and General Interest Topics** Web page include those listed below.

INTERNET SITE	ADDRESS
Career Mosaic	*http://www.CareerMosaic.com*
EINet Galaxy's Workplace Index	*http://galaxy.einet.net/galaxy/Community/Workplace.html*
NCS Career Magazine	*http://www.careermag.com/careermag/*
Online Career Center	*http://occ.com*

"Within the next decade education will change more than it has changed since the modern school was created by the printed book over three hundred years ago. An economy in which knowledge is becoming the true capital and the premier wealth-producing resource makes new and stringent demands on schools. Since learning increasingly controls access to jobs, livelihoods, and careers in the knowledge society, all members of society need to be literate. Literacy now requires a considerable understanding of technology, its dimensions, its characteristics, its rhythms—something almost totally absent today in any country."

Drucker, P.F. (1990). *The new realities in government and politics, in economics and business, in society and world view* (pp. 232-233). NY: Harper and Row.

"Science and technology have dramatically changed our perception of the world and have affected almost everything we do. The information explosion has greatly increased our understanding of the world. This revolution has also changed how we think and has led to the invention of information tools that permit us to use knowledge in new, powerful ways. Education, therefore, should be restructured to take advantage of new knowledge and new tools."

Molnar, A. (1990). Intellectual tools of the future. In J. Cash (Ed.), *The power of multimedia: A guide to interactive technology in education and business* (p. 27). Washington, DC: Interactive Video Industry Association.

"History has dealt computer and information science a special role in the inevitable restructuring of the educational system in the United States. In the coming decade, computing and information technology will be the backbone of the most significant change in education in over 100 years. Rather than being an adjunct to learning and teaching, technology is facilitating a fundamental rethinking of what should be learned and how."

Solowa, E. (1993). Reading and writing in the 21st century. *EDUCOM Review, 28* (1), 29.

"Challenging and gripping interactive computer software, dramatic narrative conveyed through electronic visual media, beautiful graphic and representational art and animation, and the rhythmic force of music all have a strong and nearly universal appeal in our culture. To improve educational outcomes by exploiting this appeal is a plausibly powerful idea. It is perhaps the most quintessential idea of American education in the late 20th century. We can envision a rapt classroom attending to a teacher exploiting an extensive visual database. But to what extent do activities like these occur on a regular basis?"

Becker, H. J. (1994). *Analysis and trends of school use of new information technologies.* (p. 1). Report to the Office of Technology Assessment. Irvine, CA: Department of Education, University of California, Irvine.

part

8

Linking Educational Psychology to Internet Resources

This section of the *Guide* provides examples of Internet resources addressing central topics in educational psychology. It is organized by topic, corresponding with the chapters in *Educational Psychology: Windows on Teaching* (Crowl et al., 1997) and *Educational Psychology: Effective Teaching, Effective Learning* (Elliott et al., 1996). Many of the Internet resources cited have broad utility and are listed on the **Internet Resources for Educators** Web page. Others are more specific resources; they are contained on the **Educational Psychology Topics** Web page, which addresses such issues as:

Perspectives on Teaching
Development of Students
Diversity in Schools & Classrooms
Learning Theories & Practices
Design and Management of Classroom Instruction
Assessing Learning & Evaluating Instruction

Thousands of resources on the Internet are pertinent to educational psychology. The examples provided are by no means exhaustive listings. The Internet is too vast for this to be possible. Rather, they are intended as "starting points" — carefully selected Internet sites that illustrate types of resources on the Internet that can be used to expand your understanding of educational psychology.

Exploring the suggested resources will enable you to expand significantly your mastery of key concepts. They were chosen because they will enhance your understanding of teaching and learning. Further, they are high quality resources helpful for defining instructional objectives, designing instructional strategies, assessing student performance, and conducting research related to educational psychology.

New materials are continually being added to the **Educational Psychology Topics** Web page — as well as the other Web pages. In this way, the **Educational Psychology Web Pages** enhance the role of the Internet as a learning laboratory which brings the most current knowledge and resources to college and university instruction.

Introduction to Educational Psychology – Perspectives on Teaching

In this section, Internet resources are examined that relate to (1) teaching and learning, (2) research and educational psychology, and (3) diversity in the classroom.

Educational Psychology: Teaching and Learning

In preparing for the teaching profession, it is important to have a clear idea of what it means to teach and what it means to learn. The Internet has many resources that help provide a rich understanding of differing perspectives on teaching and the roles of teachers.

What Does It Mean to Teach Effectively?

What do we mean by effective teaching? There are many different definitions and views of teaching. Many of these have common attributes. However, there are also important differences, such that there is not a uniform view of teachers' roles. You can learn about how different teachers view and carry out their roles by subscribing to one or more of the education listservs that involve discussions among teachers. You can participate in the exchanges among teachers that occur through these listservs using the procedures described in Part 2.

Who Becomes A Teacher?

There have been hundreds of research studies and conference proceedings on beginning teachers — those in the first few years of their professional experience. These studies and analyses have examined who our new teachers are, why they have chosen the profession, and their early teaching experiences. ERIC contains abstracts of many of these publications. To locate and read their abstracts, select ERIC on the **Internet Resources for Educators** Web page. Then use the following procedure:

1. Click on *Search ERIC Database.*
2. Enter *Beginning Teachers* as your keyword.
3. Click on Submit Query.
   Abstracts of documents in the ERIC Database will be provided to you. Any of them can be printed out. After you have reviewed the abstracts online, decide which ones will be valuable to you and print them out. Now, to continue your search or conduct another search:
4. Click on Back at the top of the page, which will return you to Search ERIC Database.
5. If you wish, conduct another search on a topic of your own designation.

Teaching and Educational Issues

Language and Literacy Instruction

There are differing opinions concerning the optimal content and methods of instruction in several areas of K-12 education. In the areas of language arts and reading, much discussion and debate centers on the topic of whole language instruction. You can learn more about these issues from documents on language and literacy in the ERIC Database. Use the Search ERIC Database procedure outlined above to obtain abstracts of studies and articles on language and literacy instruction. Use the same procedure, substituting *Language Instruction* and *Literacy Instruction* as your keywords.

Mathematics Education

During the past two decades, American students' performance in mathematics has consistently been lower than that of students from other industrial nations. Abstracts of studies on this and other key issues in mathematics education can also be found on the ERIC Database. Use *Mathematics Education* and *Mathematics Achievement* as your keywords.

The National Council of Teachers of Mathematics (NCTM) has recommended significant reforms in mathematics instruction. These include a greater focus on mathematical reasoning and communication, problem-solving, collaborative learning, and connecting and applying mathematical ideas (NCTM, 1991). Examples of lesson plans reflecting these approaches can be found in AskERIC Lesson Plans. This is a database that includes hundreds of high quality lessons in every subject. To view samples of high quality lesson plans, go to the *Lesson Plans* menu on the **Internet Resources for Educators** Web page and:

1. Click on *AskERIC Lesson Plans (Gopher).*
2. Click on *Subject Specific Lesson Plans..*
3. Click on a subject to view lesson plans in that discipline.

You will receive a list of mathematics lessons in ERIC. Click on a number of them that are of interest to you, one at a time, view them, and print out any that you think will be useful.

Science Education

As a nation, we face significant shortages in the numbers of individuals prepared to participate in our increasingly technological economy. In attempting to enhance students' understanding of and interest in science and technology, many educators have turned to active, "hands-on, minds-on" approaches to teaching these subjects.

To learn about effective approaches and programs in science education, use Search ERIC Database and enter as keywords *Science Education* and *Science Curriculum*. To obtain examples of lesson plans, use the procedure described above to access lessons from the ERIC collection using *Science* as your keyword.

Retention in Grade

Retention in grade has been an issue of considerable concern and debate during the past several years, with research suggesting that it is generally not beneficial for students. This is another topic on which the ERIC Database contains numerous up-to-date research abstracts. To access them, follow the Search ERIC Database procedures, using *Retention in Grade* as your keyword.

Homework

Research suggests that homework makes a positive contribution to students' school achievement and can help to strengthen relationships between home and school. To find abstracts of research on these issues, use the Search ERIC Database procedure with *Homework* as the keyword.

Teaching As An Art and As a Science

Many individuals have contributed to our understanding of teaching as a profession having components of both an art and a science. Others have contributed to describing the knowledge base for teaching. To find abstracts of documents on this topic, use Search ERIC Database with the keyword *Knowledge Base for Teaching*.

Culture and Schooling: Our Multicultural Classrooms

The demographics of the U.S. have changed significantly and continue to change rapidly, having important implications for K-12 education. In learning how to respond to diversity within your classroom, you will find ERIC Digests, as well as abstracts from the ERIC Bibliographic Database, on the topic of multicultural education useful. The Digests are available online and provide comprehensive and concise overviews of key issues. Examples of ERIC Digests relevant to multicultural education include:

Asian-American Children: What Teachers Should Know
Assessment of Minority Students
Communicating with Culturally Diverse Parents of Exceptional Children
Cultural Values and Motivation
Family Involvement in Early Multicultural Learning
Hispanic Parent Involvement
Literature as Lessons on the Diversity of Culture
Multicultural Education in Elementary and Secondary Schools
Multicultural Mathematics: A More Inclusive Mathematics
Self Identity and the Culturally Diverse Child
Teaching With A Multicultural Perspective

To obtain these and other ERIC Digests related to the topic of multicultural education, go to the **Databases and Informational Resources** menu on the **Internet Resources for Educators** Web page, select ERIC, and:

1. Click on AskERIC Virtual Library.
2. Click on ERIC Resources.
3. Click on *Search ERIC Digests file.*
3. Enter *Multicultural Education* as your keyword.
4. Click on Submit Query.

Teaching and Effective Schools

American Schools and Teachers: A Place Called School

During the past decade, there has been much national focus on how to better prepare teachers for their challenging roles in K-12 education. In *A Place Called School*, John Goodlad described the nature of American schools and the areas in which teachers felt prepared and ill-prepared. His other studies on U.S. education, on teacher preparation, on professional development schools, and on reforming the teaching profession have been highly influential. To learn more about his work, use Search ERIC Database, indicate that the keyword is an author, and enter *Goodlad.*

Studies of Effective Teachers and Effective Schools

There have been many studies of the attributes of effective teachers and effective schools. The ERIC Database has hundreds of abstracts of research studies on both of these topics. To find some of them, use Search ERIC Database with *Teacher Effectiveness* and *Effective Schools as* your keywords.

Total Quality Management and Its Relevance to Education

Some educators have turned to the principles of Total Quality Management as possible answers for improving the effectiveness of our schools. To find out more about Total Quality Management (TQM) in relation to education, use Search ERIC Database and enter the keywords *Total Quality Management.* To learn more about the topic in sectors other than education, use one of the World Wide Web search engines to conduct a search on this topic. To do this, go to the **Tools for Exploring the Internet** Web page, and then:

1. Select any one of the search engines that are on the menu: InfoSeek, Lycos, WebCrawler, or Yahoo.
2. The search engine will ask for your search word(s). Enter *Total Quality Management.*
   You will get a list of many items, but you will be able to identify ones that seem to have the most relevance to education or are of most interest to you.
3. Select the items that you wish to examine and click on them one-by-one to go to them.

Research and Educational Psychology

Educational research has led to significant advances in our understanding of schools, teaching and learning. Just within the past decade, there have been thousands of research studies about schooling and about learning in school and non-school settings.

The Internet has made possible immediate access to the vast body of educational research. Searching ERIC, you can find examples of many types of research methods: descriptive, correlational, comparative, experimental, and qualitative. You can find examples of studies using surveys, interviews, and observations, as well as cross-sectional, longitudinal, cross-cultural, and case study research.

Another set of resources for learning about educational research consists of listservs that are focused on research in education. You may want to subscribe to one or two of them in order to become a participant in their ongoing discussions about educational research. They all have basically similar subscription procedures. Send a message to the subscription address indicating that you would like to subscribe (SUBSCRIBE LISTNAME <YOURFIRST NAME YOURLASTNAME>). You will receive a message back giving you the discussion address for participating. The list names and subscription addresses for several active educational research listservs are given below.

LIST	LISTNAME	SUBSCRIPTION ADDRESS
AERA-Division C: Learning and Instruction	AERA-C	*listserv@asuvm.inre.asu.edu*
AERA-Division D: Measurement and Research Methodology	AERA-D	*listserv@asuvm.inre.asu.edu*
Educational Research List	ERL-L	*listserv@asuvm.inre.asu.edu*
Learning Styles Theory and Research List	EDSTYLE	*listserv@sjuvm.stjohns.edu*

There are also online journals, newsletters, and technical reports that focus on educational research. The ones described below are all accessible under *Online Journals* on the **Internet Resources for Educators** Web page.

The University of Pittsburgh's Learning Research and Development Center *Newsletter*, for example, discusses research-based teaching methods and education reform. It highlights connections between research and practice in reading, math, science, geography, history, and other subject areas. Its Gopher address is *gopher://gopher.pitt.edu:70/11/news/lrdc.*

The *Educational Research Newsletter* focuses on research related to elementary and middle school education. Topics include many that are central in the study of educational psychology. Its web address is *http://www.capecod.net/ern/ern_home.html.*

The Committee on Institutional Cooperation's CICNet is a non-profit organization that maintains a menu of electronic journals, a number of which address educational research. Overall, hundreds of electronic journals can be accessed through it. Its Gopher address is *gopher.cic.net.*

Education Policy Analysis Archives is an online journal that discusses current policy issues in education, often including research perspectives. They can both be accessed directly through the collection of online journals developed at Arizona State University (*http://seamonkey.ed.asu.edu/epaa/*).

There is a rapidly increasing number of electronic journals available via the Internet. **Electronic Texts, Journals, Newsletters, Magazines, and Collections** is a Web page that has listings of such journals, some of which are research journals pertinent to education. It is on the **Online Journals** menu on the **Internet Resources for Educators** Web page. Its direct Web address is *http://dewey.lib.ncsu.edu/stacks/index.html.*

Diversity in the Classroom: Culture, Class and Gender

As noted earlier, there has been a very substantial increase in the diversity found within American schools and classrooms during the past decade. One of the key challenges faced by all educators is to address the needs of students who vary in cultural and language background, social class and gender. Many resources on the Internet can help you better understand America's diverse student population and develop effective strategies for responding to this diversity.

The National Center for Research on Cultural Diversity and Second Language Learning, located at the University of California, Santa Cruz, has numerous valuable online resources addressing diversity. Its Web site includes, for example, many theoretical and research papers and reports related to issues of cultural and language diversity, exemplary schooling for language minority students, and bilingual education.

An example of the type of paper that is available through this site is "School Reform and Student Diversity: Exemplary Schooling for Language Minority Students," by Beverly McLeod. This report profiles schools that have been effective in implementing successful education reforms for students who are not yet proficient in English. The National Center is included under *Diversity in Schools and Classrooms* on the **Educational Psychology Topics** Web page. Its

Web address is *http://zzyx.ucsc.edu/Cntr/cntr.html.*

Diversity on the Internet is a Gopher site created by the University of Michigan as part of its Internet Resource Directory project. It includes resources that are helpful in learning about such topics as different Latino and Asian cultures and languages. Its resources address ethnic history in the U.S., immigration history, issues related to American culture, Chicano/Latino culture and literature, and the history of life in the U.S. for Asian Americans. It is included under **Diversity in Schools and Classrooms** on the **Educational Psychology Topics** Web page. Its direct Gopher address is *gopher://una.hh.lib.*

umich.edu:70/00/inetdirsstacks/diversity%3Aheise. (Select "Contents" and do a search on *Diversity.*)

Among the ERIC resources addressing student diversity are several Digests related to bilingual education. They deal with such topics as different strategies of bilingual education and current research on bilingual education. Examples of the Digests include:

Assessing Bilingual Students for Placement and Instruction
Bilingual Education for Exceptional Children
Bilingualism and the Academic Performance of Mexican American Children: The Evolving Debate

The relationship between social class and academic achievement in the U.S. has consistently been shown to be a strong one. To learn more about this important issue, use Search ERIC Database with the keyword *Social Class.*

There are differential patterns of development and school achievement in the U.S. related to gender. Using Search ERIC Database with the keywords

Sex Differences, *Sex Bias* and *Sex Stereotypes* will enable you to locate research, journal articles, and other documents addressing these issues.

Development of Students

A second major group of issues in educational psychology relate to cognitive processes and the development of students. Topics include (1) cognitive and language development, (2) psychosocial and moral development, and (3) exceptional students.

A number of listserv discussion groups focus on topics related to the development of children and adolescents. Three maintained by ERIC are focused on early childhood and primary grade education (ECENET-L), middle school education (MIDDLE-L), and school age child care (SAC-L). To subscribe to any of them, send an e-mail message as follows:

1. Prepare e-mail that says in the message body:
   SUBSCRIBE LISTNAME <YOURFIRSTNAME YOURLASTNAME>.
2. Leave the Subject blank.
3. Send the message to the subscription address:
   listserv@postoffice.cso.uiuc.edu.
4. Keep the return message, which will indicate the discussion address for sending e-mail to members of the list.
   For example, if you were Joy Class and wanted to subscribe to ECENET-L, you would type: SUBSCRIBE ECENET-L JOY CLASS.

Cognitive and Language Development

Understanding cognitive and language development in children and adolescents provides a critical framework for planning developmentally appropriate teaching and learning. Excellent information on development in the early childhood and elementary grades is available through the ERIC Clearinghouse on Elementary and Early Childhood Education. It is located on the **Educational Psychology Topics** Web page under **Development of Students**. Its Web address is *http://ericps.ed.uiuc.edu/ericeece.html.*

Additional examples of the extensive materials on the Internet pertinent to key topics in cognitive and language development are given below.

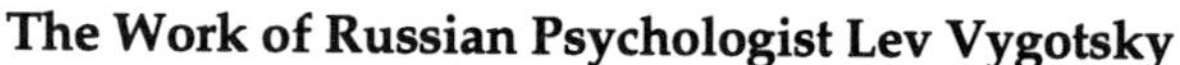

The Work of Russian Psychologist Lev Vygotsky

Lev Vygotsky was a Russian psychologist whose work contributed significantly to our understanding of the processes of development and the role of language and culture in development. A World Wide Web site addressing the work of Vygotsky is located at *http://www.massey.ac.nz/~ALock/virtual/project2.htm.*

Over 150 articles concerning Vygotsky's theory and related research are found on the ERIC database. They can be accessed by using *Vygotsky* as the keyword and designating Author as the keyword type. A few examples of the articles available are:

Everson, B. (1991). Vygotsky and the teaching of reading. *Quarterly of the National Writing Project and the Center for the Study of Writing and Literacy, 13* (3).

Mason, J., & Sinka, S. (1992). *Emerging literacy in the early childhood years: Applying a Vygotskian model of learning and development.* Urbana, IL: Center for the Study of Reading.

Royes, M. (1993). *Internalization of social discourse: A Vygotskian account of the development of young children's theories of mind.* Unpublished manuscript.

The Cognitive-Developmental Model and Contributions of Jean Piaget

Jean Piaget was a Swiss biologist, epistemologist and developmental psychologist who set forth the theory that children's development is characterized by their movement through qualitatively distinctive and hierarchically organized cognitive stages. You can identify other research related to Piaget's theory by conducting an ERIC Database search using the keywords *Piagetian Stages* and *Piagetian Theory*.

The Jean Piaget Society has an international membership of scholars, teachers and researchers interested in exploring the nature of the developmental construction of human knowledge. This group of individuals is interested in learning, researching and applying the theories of the famous Swiss psychologist and theoretician. The Jean Piaget Society Home Page is an excellent resource that includes the Jean Piaget Symposium Series, the *Genetic Epistemologist* (the journal of the Jean Piaget Society), and links to other developmental psychology sites and Internet resources.

The Jean Piaget Society Home Page can be accessed under **Development of Students** on the **Educational Psychology Topics** Web page. Its direct Web address is: *http://vanbc.wimsey.com/~chrisl/JPS/JPS.html.* To subscribe to the Jean Piaget Society (JPS) Electronic Mailing List:

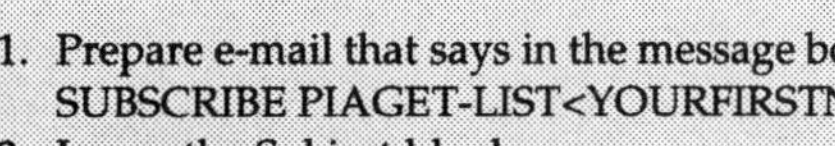

1. Prepare e-mail that says in the message body:
   SUBSCRIBE PIAGET-LIST<YOURFIRSTNAME YOURLASTNAME>.
2. Leave the Subject blank.
3. Send the message to the subscription address:
   majordomo@unixg.ubc.ca
4. Keep the return message, which will indicate the discussion address.

Developmental Stages

Materials on the Internet can broaden and enhance your understanding of children's developmental stages. Many useful articles concerning cognitive and language development are, for example, available in the ERIC database. They can be located using Search ERIC Database with the keywords *Cognitive Development, Language Development, Developmental Milestones,* and *Developmental Stages.*

Culture and Language

There are many online resources related to (a) culture and language, (b) language development among students from non-English-speaking homes, and (c) effective approaches for addressing the needs of these students are available from the **National Center for Research on Cultural Diversity and Second Language Learning.** "Moving In and Out of Bilingualism: Investigating Native Language Maintenance and Shift in Mexican-Descent Children," for example, examines language maintenance and the shift to use English among children of Mexican descent. It has important information for teachers regarding language and communication with children from non-English-speaking homes.

Social, Emotional, and Moral Development

Many resources can be found on the Internet concerning psychosocial and moral development of children and adolescents. Examples are materials pertaining to (a) the eight stages of psychosocial development described by Erik Erikson and (b) the theory of moral development proposed by Lawrence Kohlberg.

The ERIC database has abstracts of numerous journal articles and other publications about Lawrence Kohlberg's theory of moral development, his beliefs concerning moral education, and the work of other scholars whose research has extended or modified his findings. Examples include:

Harding, C., & Snyder, K. (1991). Tom, Huck, and Oliver Stone as advocates for Kohlberg's Just Community: Theory-based strategies for moral education. *Adolescence, 26* (102).
Hayes, R. (1994). The legacy of Lawrence Kohlberg: Implications for counseling and human development. *Journal of Counseling and Development, 72* (3).
Kavathatzopoulos, I. (1991). Kohlberg and Piaget: Differences and similarities. *Journal of Moral Education, 20* (1).
Krebs, D. (1994). Gender and perspective differences in moral judgment and moral orientation. *Journal of Moral Education, 23* (1).

Internet-Based Projects Relevant to Psychosocial and Moral Development

A number of Internet-based learning projects deal with social problems that are currently confronting youth and are of value in promoting their psychosocial, moral and ethical development. These projects generally use telecommunications to foster collaborative learning around important issues among students at different locations around the Nation and the world. An educator from the Montgomery County Public Schools describes the following online projects: A Comparison of Social Problems; Putting Historical Events into Perspective: Shakespeare and Mark Twain; and a Comparison of Consumer Consumption. These projects are located at Educational Projects Online, listed under *Learning Projects* on the **Internet Resources for Educators** Web page. Its Web site address is *http://pixel.cs.vt.edu/melissa/projects.html*. You will find many other online projects that have among their goals enhancing students' social and ethical reasoning and behavior.

Learner Characteristics: Exceptional Students

One of the most important challenges new teachers face is inclusion of all students — children with disabilities as well as gifted and talented students (Crowl et al., 1997). The Web search engines will lead you to many resources dealing with this area. Conducting searches on such topics as *Learning Disabilities* and *Gifted and Talented Youth* will yield references related to working with children having varying abilities.

The ERIC Database has abstracts of thousands of excellent documents concerning exceptional children. They can be accessed by using Search ERIC Database with such keywords as *Special Education, Disabilities, Gifted,* and *Mainstreaming*. ERIC also has many high quality Digests on issues pertaining to these students. Examples include the following ERIC Digests:

Challenging Gifted Students in the Regular Classroom
Disabilities: An Overview
Educating Exceptional Children
Effective Instruction for Language Minority Children with Mild Disabilities
Fostering Academic Creativity in Gifted Students
Fostering Peer Acceptance of Handicapped Students
Helping Adolescents Adjust to Giftedness
Individualized Education Program (IEP)
Learning Disabilities: Glossary of Some Important Terms
Mainstreaming
Teaching Children with Attention Deficit Disorder

Children having a range of handicaps may be mainstreamed into regular classrooms as part of the movement toward Full Inclusion. Among the discussion groups that can help teachers learn more about addressing these students' needs are ones such as the Special Needs Education Network. To subscribe to it:

1. Prepare an e-mail message that says in the message body: SUBSCRIBE SNETEACHTALK-L <YOURFIRSTNAME YOURLASTNAME>.
2. Leave the Subject blank.
3. Send the message to the subscription address: *listproc@schoolnet.carleton.ca.*

Some of the best work in the country on gifted and talented youth and educational approaches to address their needs has been done at the Johns Hopkins University Center for Talented Youth. Information about this work can be located under **Diversity in Schools and Classrooms** on the **Educational Psychology Topics** Web page or through the Web site of the Center at *http://www.jhu.edu/~gifted.*

Learning Theories and Practices

A third major set of connections between the Internet and *Educational Psychology* pertains to learning theories and practices. The connections address (1) behavioral psychology and learning, (2) cognitive psychology and learning, (3) thinking skills and problem-solving strategies, and (4) motivation in the classroom.

Behavioral Psychology and Learning

Behavioral Psychology

Behavioral psychology focuses on observable behavior and on the observable dimensions of learning. It includes attention to: patterns of behavior that are formed as a result of conditioning by external stimuli; the nature and operation of different types of reinforcement; effects of punishment on behavior; learning through modeling; techniques to increase, maintain and decrease behavior; and the application of behavioral techniques to the classroom.

ERIC has many research abstracts that pertain to behavioral psychology and learning. These abstracts can be accessed using Search ERIC Database with such keywords as *Behavior Analysis, Behavior Modification, Behaviorism, Classical Conditioning, Conditioning, Operant Conditioning,* and *Reinforcement.* In addition, an author search on *Skinner B.F.* yields abstracts of a number of analyses of the work of this leading figure in the field of behavioral psychology.

Social Cognitive Learning

Social cognitive learning relates to the processes of social learning, observational learning, and modeling. Observational learning can be enhanced by teachers' structuring classroom situations so that children learn from one another.

The foundation for much work in social cognitive learning and for related work on the topic of self-efficacy was laid by Albert Bandura (1986). Articles on these subjects can be found using Search ERIC Database with the keywords *Modeling (Psychology), Observational Learning, Self Efficacy,* and *Social Cognition.*

Research concerning cross-cultural dimensions of children's learning ways of approaching situations and solving problems can be found through a search for articles related to the work of Barbara Rogoff (1990). Use Search ERIC Database with the keywords *Rogoff Barbara* and indicate that the type of search is Author.

Cognitive Psychology, Information Processing and Learning

Cognitive psychology focuses on the role of active mental processes and mental representations in learning. It emphasizes building on students' prior knowledge and students' construction of knowledge from experience. It examines the internal processes that are used in processing information, in memory, in analysis and reflection, and in decision-making.

A good deal of information is available on the Internet on topics related to cognitive psychology, information processing, and learning. You can use Search ERIC Database and find materials on the following topics, using them as keywords:

Advance Organizers
Brain Hemisphere Functions
Cognitive Psychology
Cognitive Structures
Discovery Learning
Information Processing
Knowledge Representation
Learning Processes
Long-Term Memory
Memory
Metacognition
Perception
Recall (Psychology)
Recognition (Psychology)
Schemata (Cognition)
Short-Term Memory

By way of example, metacognition is the ability to examine one's own cognitive processes (Elliott et al., 1996, p. 269). It includes both knowledge of one's cognitive processes and intentionality in the use of cognitive strategies to enhance learning and memory. Examples of ERIC Digests on the topic of metacognition are *Developing Metacognition* and *Metacognition and Reading to Learn*.

You can acquire additional information concerning cognitive psychology and learning by conducting Web searches on these topics. Keywords yielding a number of items using one or more of the Web search engines include, for example, *Cognitive Psychology, Information Processing,* and *Memory.*

A good Web site for finding applications of cognitive psychology is **The Institute for Constructivist Theories of Learning** home page. It encourages school projects featuring active, meaningful learning and interdisciplinary curriculum activities. The site is under **Learning Theories and Practices** on the **Educational Psychology Topics** Web page; its Web address is *http://www.institute.wnyric.org/*.

Another resource relevant to cognitive learning theories and concepts is *ABC's of Teaching with Excellence*, an instructional compendium developed at the University of California, Berkeley. It is under **Learning Theories and Practices** on the **Educational Psychology Topics** Web page. Its Gopher address is *gopher://infocal.berkeley.edu:70/11/.p/otherdepts/ttips/GD.* (Although developed for higher education, it is also relevant to K-12 teaching.)

Applying Cognitive Psychology: Examples in The Teaching of History

You can find many Internet resources that demonstrate the application of principles of cognitive psychology. This is particularly the case in learning projects that are characterized by active and collaborative learning approaches.

An example relates to methods of teaching history that emphasize role-playing, simulation, and re-enactment (often referred to as "Living History"). These approaches typically focus on meaningful learning that is active and involves students in discovery.

A number of sites on the Web describe Living History projects which teach history through students' re-enactment of historical events. While it is unlikely that most classrooms can participate in Living History enactments elsewhere, teachers can get ideas for their own teaching from descriptions of Living History activities and from learning about original historical source materials available on the Internet.

Numerous Web sites contain Civil War resources, for example, that can provide a foundation for students to participate in role playing, simulation and re-enactment. **Letters from an Iowa Soldier in the Civil War,** for example, is a collection of one soldier's letters which communicate the personal tragedies associated with the War. It is listed as Living History under **Learning Theories and Practices** on the **Educational Psychology Topics** Web page. Its Web address is *http://www.ucsc.edu/civil-war-letters/home.html.*

History lesson plans contained in the ERIC collection include additional excellent illustrations of the application of principles of cognitive psychology through active learning strategies. Examples include:

American Revolution Simulation
Mini-lesson on Writing the Constitution
Mini-lesson on Civil War Role Play
U.S. History: Writing Journals Using the Oregon Trail

Intelligence and Creativity, Thinking Skills and Problem-Solving

Numerous resources at different Internet sites and on ERIC relate to intelligence and creativity, thinking skills and problem-solving strategies. Using one or more of the Web search engines or searching the ERIC Database or ERIC Digests File will identify many resources on each of these central topics in educational psychology. Keywords (topics and authors) that are useful for searches in these areas are listed below.

Costa (Arthur)	Heuristics
Creative Development	Intelligence
Creative Thinking	Perkins (David)
Creativity	Problem-Solving
Critical Thinking	Sternberg (Robert)
Cultural Influences	Thinking Skills
Educational Objectives	Transfer of Learning
Gardner (Howard)	Visualization

Critical Thinking

Fostering critical thinking on the part of students is a fundamental objective of many educators. It has been defined by cognitive psychologist Robert Sternberg as comprising "the mental processes, strategies, and representations people use to solve problems, make decisions, and learn new concepts" (Sternberg, 1985). Examples of the many materials on the Internet that relate to fostering critical thinking among students include the following ERIC Digests:

Critical Thinking in the Social Studies
Critical Thinking: Promoting It in the Classroom
Critical Thinking in College English Studies
Teaching Critical Thinking Through Environmental Education

The ERIC Database has abstracts for many publications on the topic of critical thinking. Instructional resources on this topic can also be found at other sites on the Internet, two good examples of which are cited here. The *Critical Thinking Community Home Page* is listed under **Learning Theories and Practices** on the **Educational Psychology Topics** Web page. Its Web address is *http://loki.sonoma.edu/cthink/.* The direct Web address for *Critical Thinking Lessons,* also listed under **Learning Theories and Practices,** is *http://execpc.com:80/~dboals/K-12.html.*

Problem-Solving

Most educators are concerned with improving students' abilities to solve problems at school and with fostering application of these skills outside the classroom. A substantial number of the learning projects on the Internet are designed to foster problem-solving. NASA K12 Projects, for example, focus on students solving problems that relate to space science. These include problems related to conducting scientific investigations, guiding satellites, and living in space. It is listed under *Learning Projects* on the **Instructional Resources** section of the **Internet Resources for Educators** Web page. Its direct Web address is *http://quest.arc.nasa.gov.*

Motivation in the Classroom

Motivation is one of the critical keys to learning. Research tells us conclusively that it has a significant effect on learning outcomes and on students' decisions about their educational choices. ERIC has hundreds of documents concerning motivation in the ERIC Bibliographic Database and the ERIC Digests File. Among the pertinent ERIC Digests are:

Empowering Culturally and Linguistically Diverse Students with Learning Problems
Empowering Young Black Males
Fostering the Postsecondary Aspirations of Gifted Urban Minority Students
Motivating American Indian Students in Science and Math
Motivating the Mexican American Student
Praise in the Classroom

You can find many suggestions from Great Britain of motivating curriculum activities that derive from a British tradition of child-centered education that builds on students' natural learning. Central aims are for learning activities to be intrinsically interesting for students and to have assessment incorporated in a natural way. Primary grade curriculum activities in one project included such experiences as:

Designing a finger puppet
Meeting an unusual centipede and planning its lunch
Collecting data on known puppets
Planning and producing a simple puppet show
Looking for and describing shadows
Watching the changing shape and position of shadows

Projects such as this are found in *Student-Centered Learning: Examples from Great Britain,* under **Learning Theories and Practices** on the **Educational Psychology Topics** Web page. Its Web address is *http://acorn.educ.nottingham.ac.uk.*

Cooperative Learning

Cooperative learning refers to instructional methods in which students are encouraged or required to work together on academic tasks, helping one another to learn (Slavin, 1991). Many cooperative learning activities for use by individual K-12 classrooms and many collaborative projects for classrooms communicating via telecommunications are described on the Internet.

A substantial number of high quality documents concerning cooperative learning are available through ERIC. They examine cooperative learning theories, approaches for implementing cooperative learning, and benefits of these approaches for students. Examples include abstracts of numerous publications on cooperative learning as well as such ERIC Digests as:

Cooperative Learning Strategies and Children
Cooperative Learning in the Urban Classroom
Cooperative Learning for Students from Diverse Language Backgrounds
Cooperative Learning in Social Studies Education: What Does the Research Say?
Cooperative Learning with Limited-English-Proficient Students

Design and Management of Classroom Instruction: Shaping the Learning Environment

Another major group of connections between the Internet and *Educational Psychology* pertain to design and management of classroom instruction. They focus on (1) planning for essential learning outcomes, (2) effective teaching strategies and the design of instruction, and (3) classroom management, organization and control.

Instructional Planning for Essential Learning Outcomes

Clearly specifying goals and objectives are essential for planning instruction and for achieving the learning outcomes we desire. At the classroom level, the starting point of well-designed instruction for a lesson, a unit, or a course, is carefully defined objectives and learning outcomes.

Educational Standards

The National Goals 2000 initiative has involved individuals from across the U.S. and has resulted in the establishment of national goals for K-12 education and standards for each of the academic disciplines. The Standards and Benchmarks Database is maintained by the MidContinent Regional Educational Laboratory. It is listed under **Design and Management of Classroom Instruction** on the **Educational Psychology Topics** Web page. Its Web address is *http://mcrel.org/standards-benchmarks/.*

The U.S. Department of Education has created a comprehensive database on Goals 2000. It includes documents and reports related to the National goals, the progress that has been made in achieving them, and the resources that are available for helping educators to address them. Its Web address is *http://www.ed.gov/G2k/*. It is located on the **Educational Psychology Topics** Web page under **Perspectives on Teaching**.

There has been a considerable amount of federal legislation on the issues of Goals 2000 and educational standards. You can find out about recent legislative initiatives through the Congressional Legislation Web site, **Thomas**. It is located under **Additional Information Sources** on the **Internet Resources for Educators** Web page.

Defining Educational Objectives and Learner Outcomes

Educational objectives are the critical starting point for instruction. They help answer such central questions as: How do you define your teaching as successful? What are your students expected to learn? What do you want your students to accomplish in a particular lesson, a unit, and a course?

A number of Internet resources can help you develop an understanding of the role of educational objectives. A good starting point is again the ERIC Database. Enter *Educational Objectives* and *Outcomes of Education* as keywords in your search. You will be given abstracts of articles and papers that relate to these topics.

The Role of Objectives in Instruction

The educational objectives teachers establish for their classes provide direction for their instructional planning, teaching, and assessment (Elliott et al., 1996). They are written in terms of student outcomes.

A search of the ERIC Lesson Plan collection, accessible through the **Internet Resources for Educators** Web page, will enable you to develop a further understanding of the role of objectives in instruction, how to develop them, and how to connect them with instructional content. It will be valuable for you to conduct a search of **ERIC Lesson Plans** choosing a few different subjects in order to develop a sense of well-formulated educational objectives.

In establishing educational objectives, it is important to have high expectations for students of all backgrounds. To examine issues related to educational goals and objectives for students from diverse backgrounds, use Search ERIC Database with the following authors as keywords:

Banks (James)
Comer (James)
Garcia (Eugene)
Levin (Henry)
Nieto (Sonia)

Each of these individuals has contributed significantly to our understanding of the value of challenging objectives for students from all cultural, language and socioeconomic groups.

Effective Teaching Strategies and the Design of Instruction

Resources demonstrating a wide range of teaching strategies and instructional designs can be found on the Internet. The examples given below have been chosen to illustrate a few of the types of materials on the Internet relevant to effective teaching.

Inquiry Learning and Teaching

Teaching that encourages inquiry learning has received favorable attention over many years. This is due to its conformity with fundamental principles of learning and the success many teachers have experienced with this approach. A large number of abstracts in the ERIC Database address inquiry learning. To locate them, conduct searches on the keywords *Active Learning, Discovery Learning, Exploratory Learning, Inquiry,* and *Learning Centers (Classroom).*

References and resources concerning inquiry-based learning are also found in *inQuiry Almanac.* It is a monthly online magazine for educators designed to foster use of the Internet for inquiry-based teaching. It can be accessed under **Online Journals** on the **Internet Resources for Educators** Web page. Its Web address is *http://sln.fi.edu./qanda/qanda.html.*

Parents' Involvement in Students' Learning

Benefits of parent involvement in students' learning and ways of enhancing parent's roles in their children's education are discussed in many documents on the Internet.

The **U.S. Department of Education** has made available a series of *Helping Your Child* pamphlets which contain useful suggestions for teachers as well as parents. They are available under **Design and Management of Classroom Instruction** on the **Educational Psychology Topics** Web page.

Helping Your Child Learn Math: Parent Involvement Materials suggests activities for parents to help them stimulate their children's interest in math. Its focus is on children from 5-13 years of age. It is on the U.S.

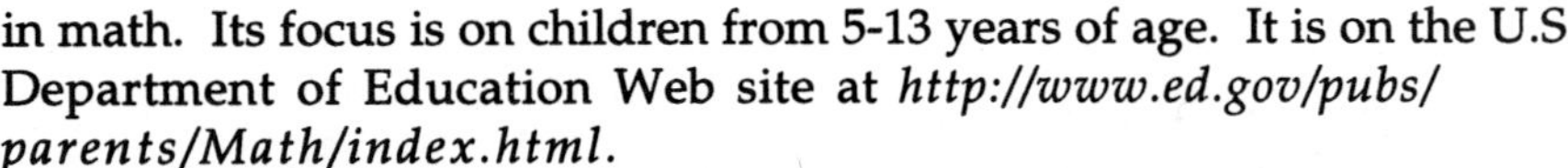

Department of Education Web site at *http://www.ed.gov/pubs/parents/Math/index.html.*

Helping Your Child Learn Science: Parent Involvement Materials suggests activities for parents to help them stimulate an interest in science. Its focus is on children from 3-10 years of age. Its Department of Education Web address is *http://www.ed.gov/pubs/parents/Science/index.html.*

The remaining pamphlets in the *Helping Your Child Learn* series address other subject areas as well as helping children with homework, to write well, to learn responsible behavior, to succeed in school, and in test taking. The Department of Education Web address where they are located is *http://www.ed.gov/pubs/parents.html*

An example of a Parent Teacher Association (PTA) resource on parental roles in children's education is *Texas PTA Parent Involvement Initiatives.* It identifies steps parents can take at home and in interaction with the school to enhance their children's success in school. It is available under **Design and Management of Classroom Instruction** on the **Educational Psychology Topics** Web page. Its Web address is *http://www.onr.com/tpta/parent.html.*

Teacher Expectations and Learning

Teacher expectations have a substantial influence on students' learning and achievement. Many references included on the ERIC Database address this issue, and you can locate them using the keywords *Self-Fulfilling Prophecies, Teacher Expectations of Students,* and *Teacher Influence.* The materials discuss the marked impacts of teacher expectations and the positive benefits on student performance of their teacher's belief that they can learn at high levels. Examples of the references include:

Metcalf, L. (1995). Great expectations: How changing your thinking can change your students. *Learning,* 23, 93-95.
Shakeshaft, C. (1995). Reforming science education to include girls. *Theory into Practice,* 34, 74-79.

Classroom Management and Organization

Classroom Management and Discipline

Managing a classroom means establishing routines that enable learning to proceed smoothly and that help to prevent unnecessary discipline problems (Elliott et al., 1996, p. 434). It requires understanding of different management techniques and consists of a range of skills that are critical for new teachers to be successful.

The ERIC Bibliographic Database and ERIC Digests have a substantial number of references on issues related to classroom management. Examples of the ERIC Digests on the topic of classroom management are:

Praise in the Classroom
Positive Discipline
Managing Inappropriate Behavior in the Classroom
Student Discipline Policies

Classroom Climate, Organization and Control

It will be valuable for you to learn about the journal articles and other publications on classroom climate, organization and control on the ERIC Database. You can do this by performing Search ERIC Database using the keywords *Classroom Communication, Classroom Climate, Classroom Discipline, Classroom Environment, Classroom Management, Student Behavior,* and *Time Management.* You will find articles on such topics as: practical steps in classroom management for beginning teachers; how to create a positive classroom environment that prevents discipline problems; how to deal with disruptive students; and how to carefully manage time use in the classroom.

Teaching and Educational Technology

The Internet offers extensive resources on how to locate, use and integrate technology into instructional practices. Many of these focus on ways in which technology can be used to significantly enhance instruction by creating authentic, challenging learning experiences for students, fostering collaborative learning, and enabling the teacher to serve as a facilitator of learning (Means et al., 1993).

A good way to begin exploring these resources is with a search of documents concerning technology in education available on the **U.S. Department of Education** Web page. Select *Secretary's Initiatives* and then choose *Technology*. This will take you to a list of excellent current reports and references. These documents are also available under **Design and Management of Classroom Instruction** on the **Educational Psychology Topics** Web page. Their direct Web address is *http://www.ed.gov.*

The ERIC Clearinghouse on Information and Technology is another valuable source for exploring teaching and technology. It contains resources concerning computers, telecommunications, CD-ROM, multimedia, and all aspects of educational technology. It is under **Design and Management of Classroom Instruction** on the **Educational Psychology Topics** Web page. Its direct Web address is *http://ericir.syr.edu/ithome/.*

How Technology is Being Used in Classrooms

Searching the Internet for resources related to teaching and technology by using the Web search engines will yield many different materials. The following are examples of links to Internet resources, identified by search engines, that relate to use of technology in K-12 teaching:

Educational Technology Initiatives (UK/Wales/Ireland)
Global Schoolhouse Gopher
Technical Education Research Center
Technology and Information Educational Services (TIES)
Virtual Schoolhouse (K-12)
SchoolNet Gopher
SciLinkGopher

Each of the Web search engines has links to many sites that relate to uses of technology in K-12 teaching. Sites to which search engines have links related to science education include, for example:

Astronomical Pictures and Animations
Current Weather Maps
The Daily Planet
NASA Information Sites
Safari Splash! Newsletter
Science Resources
Weather Information OnLine: Weather Machine

Learning Activities Integrating Technology into Instruction

Many lesson plans which integrate technology into teaching are available on the Internet. The **ERIC Lesson Plans** collection, for example, includes on its menu *Technology Lesson Plans.* This contains a large number of lessons that use technology in learning in a wide variety of ways.

Academy One has links to a large number of educational projects using technology in teaching. In addition, it has links to sites that provide suggestions and facilitate the use of the Internet as an instructional resource. Examples of projects and resources include:

Dinosaurs
Exploring Science for Kids
Frog Dissection
Louvre Museum
The White House
NASA for Kids
NASA - Planets Pictures
US Civil War Center
MegaMath Project
Newspapers: USA and Selected Countries

Multimedia Resources

A large number of resources related to using multimedia, laser videodiscs, and CD-ROMs are available on the Internet. The ERIC Clearinghouse on Information and Technology includes many materials aimed at helping teachers use computer and multimedia materials to enhance the quality of teaching and learning. It is accessible through the **Internet Resources for Educators** Web page. It can also be reached through AskERIC via e-mail (*askeric@ericir.syr.edu*) or through the AskERIC Virtual Library.

The largest producer of multimedia videodiscs for K-12 education is Optical Data Corporation. The majority of its videodiscs are in science and mathematics and are bilingual in English and Spanish. Research concerning their effectiveness is available on Optical Data's Web page, which is accessible under **Design and Management of Classroom Instruction** on the **Educational Psychology Topics** Web page. The direct Web address is *http://www.opticaldata.com/*.

Selecting Internet Resources for Your Classroom

In selecting and integrating technology-based instructional materials into your teaching, it is important to have sound criteria to guide your choices. This is particularly true for Internet resources, which are being introduced rapidly, often with little or no previous pilot-testing. A document providing useful guidelines is part of *Pathways to School Improvement*, a project which has developed extensive materials pertinent to high quality instruction (it is administered by the North Central Regional Educational Laboratory). *Critical Issue: Locating, Using and Integrating Internet-Based Mathematics Materials*, is one of many excellent analyses accessible under **Design and Management of Classroom Instruction** on the **Educational Psychology Topics** Web page. The *Pathways to School Improvement* Web address is *http://www.ncrel.org/*.

Listserv Discussions of Educational Technologies

A number of listservs are focused specifically on technology and teaching. You might consider subscribing to one or more of those listed below.

EDNET is a list that explores the educational potential of the Internet. FIELD TRIPS links K-12 classes to hundreds of other students in the U.S. and abroad. IECC — International E-mail Classroom Connections — is a virtual meeting place for teachers seeking partner classes for international and cross-cultural e-mail exchanges. INCLASS is one of many listservs operated through Canada's SchoolNet. KIDSPHERE is a very active listserv which features discussions about numerous aspects of bringing technology into the classroom. WWWEDU — the World Wide Web in Education — is a discussion group of more than 1,000 educators around the world who share ideas on how to use the Web in K-12 classrooms.

LIST	LISTNAME	SUBSCRIPTION ADDRESS
Consortium for School Networking	COSNDISC	*listproc@list.cren.net*
EDNET	EDNET	*listproc@lists.umass.edu*
Fieldtrips	FIELDTRIPS-L	*majordomo@gsn.org**
International Email Classroom Connections	IECC	*iecc-request@stolaf.edu*
INCLASS (SCHOOLNET)	INCLASS	*listproc@schoolnet.carleton.ca*
KIDSPHERE	KIDSPHERE	*kidsphere-request@vms.cis.pitt.edu*
World Wide Web in Education	WWWEDU	*listproc@educom.unc.edu*

*Indicate your e-mail address (rather than your name) in the message after SUBSCRIBE FIELDTRIPS-L.

Assessing Student Learning and Evaluating Instruction

Principles of Measurement, Assessment and Evaluation

Another important set of linkages between the Internet and *Educational Psychology* relate to principles of measurement, assessing means of learning and evaluation of instruction. Among the key areas addressed are (1) informal assessment, teacher-constructed tests and authentic assessment methods and (2) formal assessment, standardized tests and rating scales.

Informal Evaluation, Teacher-Constructed Testing and Authentic Assessment

As a teacher, you will be involved in constructing classroom tests and assessment instruments. To learn more about teacher-constructed tests and performance assessment, often referred to as *authentic assessment*, you can search the ERIC Database using such keywords as *Authentic Assessment, Performance Assessment, Portfolio Assessment* and *Teacher-Made Tests.* Use these keywords alone or with a designated subject area or grade level.

For example, conducting a search with *Authentic Assessment* and *Elementary Schools* as keywords generates such abstracts as:

Falk, B. (1994). The Bronx New School: *Weaving assessment into the fabric of teaching and learning. A series on authentic assessment and accountability.* NY: Columbia University, Teachers College, National Center for Restructuring Education, Schools and Teaching.

Lockwood, A. (1991). Authentic assessment. *Focus in Change, Newsletter of the National Center for Effective Schools, 3* (1).

Paris, S., & Ayres, L. (1994). *Becoming reflective students and teachers with portfolios and authentic assessment. Psychology in the classroom: A series on applied educational psychology.* Washington, DC: American Psychological Association.

You can get suggestions for constructing classroom tests from such ERIC Digests as *Constructing Classroom Achievement Tests, Open-Ended Questions in Reading,* and *Integrating Testing with Teaching.* You can locate examples of teacher-constructed assessment materials in various subject areas and grade levels by reviewing lesson plans in the ERIC collection. You can learn more about grading and reporting student performance by reading publications found in the ERIC Database using the keywords *Grading* and *Report Cards.*

Performance or "Authentic" Assessment Methods

Many materials concerning performance or "authentic assessment" are available on the Internet. There are a number of ERIC Digests, for example, on key issues related to performance and authentic assessment, as described below.

Performance Assessment. This Digest gives a concise overview of performance assessment, how it is used, why it is valuable, what research says about its effects, and what it costs, as well as examples of successful performance assessment programs.

Authentic Mathematics Assessment. This is a discussion of current ideas and practices related to performance assessment in mathematics. Types of assessment items described include open-ended questions, short investigations, multiple choice questions emphasizing understanding, and portfolios.

Authentic Writing Assessment. This Digest describes current ideas concerning authentic writing assessment, the format for an authentic writing assessment, and an example of an authentic writing program.

The Portfolio and Its Use: Developmentally Appropriate Assessment of Young Children. This is a discussion of how portfolios can be used to provide developmentally appropriate assessment of children in the early childhood and primary grades.

Research Addressing Current Issues in Assessment

The National Center for Research on Evaluation, Standards and Student Testing (CRESST), located at the Center for the Study of Evaluation (CSE) at UCLA, contains many online documents pertaining to current issues in assessment. Its *General Interest Papers* include, for example:

Teacher Changes in Beliefs, Instruction, and Assessment
Effects of Performance Assessments on Teachers and Students
Performance Assessment and Parents

CRESST's *Technical Reports* include information and ideas for using authentic assessment techniques in the classroom that are based upon current research. Examples include:

Davinroy, K., Bliem, C., & Mayfield, V. (1995). *"How does my teacher know what I know?," Third graders' perceptions of mathematics, reading and assessment.* CSE Technical Report 395.
Flexer, R., Cumbo, K., Borko, H., Mayfield, V., & Marion, S. (1995). *How "messing about" with performance assessment in mathematics affects what happens in classrooms.* CSE Technical Report 396.
Herman, J., Klein, D., Health, T., & Wakai, S. (1994). *A first look: Are claims for alternative assessment holding up?* CSE Technical Report 391.

The *CRESST Line Newsletter* also provides useful information online concerning performance assessment. Its recent issues have included, for example:

Getting Assessment Right
Implementing Performance Assessments in the Classroom
Special Portfolio Issue

CRESST also has a semi-annual publication, *Evaluation Comment,* which it provides online. Recent issues have focused on:

What Works in Performance Assessment
Portfolio Assessment: Whose Work Is It?
Assessment Questions: Equity Answers

CRESST is located under **Assessing Learning and Evaluating Instruction** on the **Educational Psychology Topics** Web page. Its Web address is

http://www.cse.ucla.edu.

The Northwest Regional Educational Laboratory, working in collaboration with CRESST, maintains such alternative assessment databases as the *Alternative Assessment in Science and Mathematics Database.* The databases contain comprehensive bibliographies of materials related to authentic assessment. Among its broad range of resources, the Laboratory maintains other alternative assessment information. It is listed under **Assessing Learning and Evaluating Instruction** on the **Educational Psychology**

Topics Web page. Its Web address is *http://www.nwrel.org/.*

The North Central Regional Educational Laboratory is another federally supported resource containing useful online materials on assessment. Its essays on *Assessment Issues,* for example, are thorough analyses which include attention to assessment in relation to theories of learning. Examples include:

What Does Research Say About Assessment? This is a comprehensive paper about performance-based assessment, its relationship to cognitive views of learning, and issues of equity in assessment.

Why Should Assessment Be Based on A Vision of Learning? This paper provides a model of multidimensional assessment which is broad-based, relevant to real life, and uses a multiplicity of measures which provide a rich portrait of students' learning.

The Laboratory is on the **Educational Psychology Topics** Web page under **Assessing Learning and Evaluating Instruction**. Its Web address is

http://www.ncrel.org/.

Standardized Tests and Rating Scales in the Classroom

The Internet provides access to many resources related to standardized tests and rating scales. The ERIC Clearinghouse on Assessment and Evaluation is a particularly valuable resource to enhance understanding of standardized assessment procedures. It contains a guide to assessment information on the Internet and links to assessment materials at other federally supported sites. It also contains the databases described below, as well as such helpful online documents as *Test Selection Tips.*

Test and Test Review Locator Database

The ERIC Clearinghouse on Assessment and Evaluation contains the "Test Locator" database, which references over 10,000 tests in education. It includes virtually all fields of education and includes educational achievement, aptitude and attitude tests, and measurements. The Clearinghouse also contains the "Buros Test Review Locator" and provides access to the Educational Testing Service (ETS) Test Collection.

The Test and Test Review Locator are extremely valuable for a number of activities. These include: locating tests matched to particular purposes; learning details about them; and determining their appropriate uses, the settings for which they are designed, and the guidelines for administering, scoring, and interpreting them. The ERIC Clearinghouse on Assessment and Evaluation is located under **Assessing Learning and Evaluation Instruction** on the **Educational Psychology Topics** Web page. Its direct Web address is *http://www.cua.edu/www/eric_ae.*

Standardized Tests and Rating Scales and Their Uses

The ERIC Bibliographic Database has abstracts of hundreds of journal articles and other publications concerning standardized tests and rating scales and their uses. Keywords for locating these materials follow.

Achievement Tests	Scoring
Aptitude Tests	Standardized Tests
Educational Testing	Test Norms
Intelligence Tests	Test Reliability
Norm Referenced Tests	Test Selection
Objective Tests	Test Validity
Rating Scales	Test Wiseness
Screening Tests	Tests

CRESST, described earlier, also provides materials pertinent to standardized testing and rating scales. Many of its technical reports and those of the UCLA Center for the Study of Evaluation (where it is located) are focused on standardized tests and measurement of student achievement.

K-12 Assessment Listserv Discussion Group

Learning to select, use and interpret both standardized tests and authentic assessment procedures are demanding tasks requiring experience. A good way to become informed about key issues in testing and assessment is to participate in the listserv maintained by the ERIC Clearinghouse on Assessment and Evaluation devoted to this topic. The listserv, K12ASSESS-L, uses the subscription address: *mailserv@lists.cua.edu.* To subscribe, fill out the form that is located at *http://www.cua.edu/www/eric_ae/k12assess/sub.html.* Type in your full name at *Your Full Name.* Type in your e-mail address at *Your Email address.* Click the *Subscribe* button to send in your subscription request. This is an active listserv and will provide you with many insights, tips, and issues to consider in testing and assessing the outcomes of teaching and learning.

References

Bandura, A. (1986). *Social foundations of thought and action: A social-cognitive theory.* Englewood Cliffs, NJ: Prentice Hall.

Crowl, T., Kaminsky, S. and Podell, D.M. (1997). *Educational psychology: Windows on teaching.* Dubuque, IA: Times Mirror Higher Education Group.

Elliott, S., Kratochwill, T., Littlefield, J., & Travers, J. (1996). *Educational psychology: Effective teaching, effective learning* (2nd ed.). Dubuque, IA: Times Mirror Higher Education Group.

Goodlad, J. (1984). *A place called school.* New York: McGraw-Hill.

National Council of Teachers of Mathematics. (1991). *Professional standards for teaching mathematics.* Reston, VA: Author.

Rogoff, B. (1990). *Apprenticeship in thinking.* New York: Oxford University Press.

Slavin, R. (1991). Cooperative learning and group contingencies. *Journal of Behavioral Education, 1* (1).

Sternberg, R. (1985). Critical thinking. In F. Link (Ed.), *Essays on the intellect.* Alexandria, VA: Association for Supervision and Curriculum Development.

U.S. Department of Education. (1994). *Strong families, strong schools: Building community partnerships for learning. A research base for family involvement in learning from the U.S. Department of Education.* Washington, DC: Author.

site index

E-Mail Addresses

Gopher Addresses

World Wide Web Addresses

glossary

Bulletin Board Systems (BBSs) Electronic forums for users to browse, post and exchange information. BBSs are accessible via a computer, modem, and phone line directly or via the Internet.

Electronic Mail (e-mail) The exchange of communications — the sending and receiving of messages — among individuals using computers and modems. E-mail does not require the Internet, but is frequently sent and received using it as the mode of transmission.

Frequently Asked Questions (FAQ) Many locations on the Internet have FAQ files that contain answers to frequently asked questions related to the Internet and the site.

Gopher A uniform menu-based search and retrieval system for browsing and downloading text and binary files (e.g., for pictures) on the Internet. Gopher sites provide links to other Gopher sites, yielding rapid access to thousands of sites worldwide.

Internet The Internet is an international network of computer networks originally created by the federal government and now serving educational, government, commercial and military institutions as well as millions of individuals worldwide. Gateways that convert formats and protocols between networks make the Internet function as a single network with interconnectivity among all of its parts.

Mailing Lists (listservs) Often called discussion lists, these are e-mail based online discussion groups focused on a particular topic. E-mail messages are sent by subscribers to a list's e-mail address and are then re-broadcast to all of the list subscribers.

Modem An electronic device that connects to your computer and is used to link your computer to other computers and services via phone lines.

Usenet Newsgroups Collections of messages posted by individuals on particular subjects. Messages are accessed online at the Usenet site rather than being deposited in individual user's e-mail mailbox.

Universal Resource Locator (URL) The addressing protocol used to locate specific resources on the World Wide Web. If the beginning (preface) of an address is *http://* (HyperText Transfer Protocol), this indicates that the address is for a World Wide Web site and that a Web browser, such as Netscape, will access it. The address itself is referred to as a URL.

World Wide Web (WWW) The World Wide Web is a user-friendly interface enabling the user to access millions of sources of information located on the Internet through a Web browser such as Netscape and through Web search engines. Web documents are written in "hypertext," a system that allows for text and graphical "links" to documents and files spread across the Internet.

general references

The Internet, Technology, and K-12 Education

The following is a selected list of references that deal with the Internet and include materials pertinent to K-12 applications of the Internet and educational technologies.

Books Focused on the Internet

The following are examples of several reference books that provide comprehensive overviews of the Internet. Most include information specifically relevant to K-12 education.

Drol, E. (1994). *The whole Internet: User's guide & catalog*. (2nd ed.). Sebastopol, CA: O'Reilly & Associates, Inc.

Ellsworth, J. H. (1994). *Education on the Internet.* Indianapolis, IN: Sams Publishing.

Frazier, D., Kurshan, B., & Armstrong, S. (1995). *Internet for kids.* San Francisco, CA: SYBEX.

Giagnocavo, G., McLain, T., DiStefano, W., & Sturm, C. N. (Ed.). (1995). *Educator's Internet companion.* Lancaster, PA: Wentworth Worldwide Media, Inc.

Giagnocavo, G., McLain, T., DiStefano, W., & Sturm, C. N. (Ed.). (1996). *Educator's World Wide Web tour guide.* Lancaster, PA: Wentworth Worldwide Media, Inc.

Joseph, L. (1995). *World link: An Internet guide for educators, parents, and students.* Columbus, OH: Original Works/Greyden Press.

Miller, E. B. (1995). *Internet resource directory for K-12 teachers and librarians.* Englewood, CO: Libraries Unlimited.

Magazines and Newsletters

The items listed below are examples of publications that provide practical information that is helpful in staying current on the state of the Internet in relation to K-12 teaching.

Classroom Connect — This monthly newsletter aims to help educators bring the Internet and other electronic resources into the K-12 classroom. Subscription address: Classroom Connect, Wentworth Worldwide Media, 1866 Colonial Village Lane, P.O. Box 10488, Lancaster, PA 17605-9981. E-mail address: connect@wentworth.com.

Electronic Learning: The Magazine for Technology and School Change — This magazine, published eight times a year, focuses on using technology in K-12 teaching. Subscription address: Electronic Learning, P.O. Box 53797, Boulder, CO 80322.

T.H.E. (Technological Horizons in Education) Journal — This monthly magazine is free to college and university faculty and to K-12 school administrators, computer coordinators, and department chairs. Subscription address: T.H.E. Journal, Circulation Dept., 150 El Camino Real, Suite 112, Tustin, CA 92680-3670.